COUNTRY
WOODWORKING

COUNTRY
WOODWORKING

OVER THIRTY-FIVE EASY-TO-MAKE ACCENT PIECES

Woodworking Designs by Mary Jane Favorite
Written by Nick Engler

Sedgewood® Press
New York

Dear Crafter:

Thank you for selecting *Country Woodworking*. We know you'll enjoy this collection of easy-to-make country-style accent pieces, many of which are reproductions of hard-to-find antiques.

With a minimum of tools and the expert instructions in this book, you can bring an authentic touch of country to every room of your home. The projects include small items and large ones, simple designs and those more challenging; there are decorative objects both plain and fancy, pieces that are practical, and those that are whimsical — some that even combine whimsy and usefulness.

We at Sedgewood® Press are very proud to bring you craft books of the highest quality. Our books offer a range of projects for every level of crafting skill and a wide variety of designs and uses. They feature large color photos of all projects, accurate step-by-step instructions, and clear, readable charts and diagrams.

We hope you'll be spending many pleasant hours crafting from *Country Woodworking*, and that you will look forward to other books from Sedgewood.

Cordially,

Barbara S. Machtiger
Editorial Project Manager
Sedgewood® Press

❖ ❖

For Sedgewood® Press

Director: Elizabeth P. Rice
Editorial Project Manager: Barbara S. Machtiger
Production Manager: Bill Rose
Photo Art Director: Remo Cosentino
Color Photography: Douglas Mellor

Copyright 1990 by Bookworks, Inc.

Distributed by Meredith Corporation
ISBN: 0-696-02333-4
Library of Congress Catalog Card Number: 89-061409
Printed in the United States of America
10 9 8 7 6 5 4 3 2 1

Design by Linda Watts
Packaged by Bookworks, Inc.

Special Thanks to Englewood Lumber, Englewood, Ohio.

Contents

Country Woodworking:
A Primer

efore you begin to build these projects, pause and reflect: "Country" is much more than a style of woodworking; it's a rich heritage. The roots stretch back hundreds of years, to the very beginning of this nation.

Right from the start, we were a colony of woodworkers. The English settled this land for its trees — they wanted the wood to build a mighty navy. In the New World, they found tall, straight firs for masts, sturdy oaks for hulls, and pine for waterproofing pitch. A peculiar seventeenth-century English law, the Tunnage Acts, even required that any ship going to America carry at least one trained craftsman who could work wood. So many of the first settlers who arrived in the 1600s were carpenters, cabinetmakers, coopers, bodgers, turners, and woodworkers of all descriptions.

The first American woodworking projects — chests, benches, and tables — were simple and practical. Seventeenth-century colonial craftsmen did not have the time to make fancy articles; they were too busy trying to survive. Nor did they have the appropriate tools. All they brought from the Old World were the basic carpentry and shipbuilding tools necessary for survival.

As the American colonies became more settled, some craftsmen had more time and could import better tools. Those living in the developing American cities began to make highly worked furniture and other fancy wooden pieces for the growing middle and upper classes. But those in rural areas or the frontier, where life was tenuous and the tools dear, continued to make simple, practical wooden items out of necessity.

After the first English colonists came waves of immigrants of all nationalities. Some settled in the cities, but most sought their own land to farm. Each new wave brought its own craftsmen and woodworking traditions. The newly arrived woodworkers traded ideas with those who had already settled. They began to mix styles and designs, creating many beautiful new forms.

However, the hard reality of life in rural America molded these forms as it had molded the woodworking designs of the original colonists. A typical wooden piece might be ingeniously conceived, skillfully worked, and gaily painted. But, by and large, the designs remained simple to build and practical to use. It's this endearing simplicity and practicality that was — and remains today — the heart of American country woodworking.

Woodworking Tools

Basic tools. In keeping with country woodworking tradition, we've designed the projects in this book to be built with simple, basic tools. You don't need a fully equipped woodworking shop, although you can use large power tools if you have them. At a minimum, you should have the following:

Hand Tools
Tape measure
Combination square
Combination handsaw (for both ripping and crosscutting)
Coping saw
Small (12 oz.) hammer
Nail punch
Blade screwdrivers (with 3/16" and 1/4" blades)
Phillips screwdrivers (sizes #1 and #2)
Chisels (1/4", 1/2", and 3/4")
Pocket knife
Sharpening stone (to sharpen the chisels and knife)
Half-round file
Half-round rasp
File card (to clean the file and rasp)
Pliers
Needle-nose pliers
Hand screw clamps (two 4" and two 8")

Power Tools and Accessories
Electric drill with a 3/8" chuck
Drill stand
General-purpose speed bits (1/16" to 3/8")
Wood-boring (spade) bits (3/8" to 1")
Screw drills (#6, #8, and #10)
Saber saw
Saber saw table
Saber saw blades (an assortment for both finish and regular cuts)

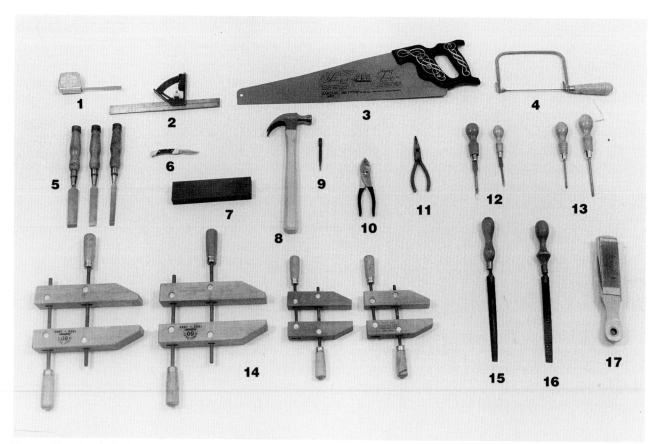

You need hand tools for four different types of woodworking operations — cutting, assembly, and shaping and finishing. The necessary *measuring* tools are (1) a tape measure and (2) a combination square. The *cutting* tools are (3) a handsaw, (4) a coping saw, (5) chisels, (6) a pocket knife, and (7) a sharpening stone.

The *assembly* tools are (8) a hammer, (9) nail punch, (10) pliers, (11) needle-nose pliers, (12) blade screwdrivers, (13) phillips screwdrivers, and (14) hand screw clamps. The *finishing and shaping* tools are (15) a file, (16) a rasp, and (17) a file card.

COUNTRY WOODWORKING:
A PRIMER

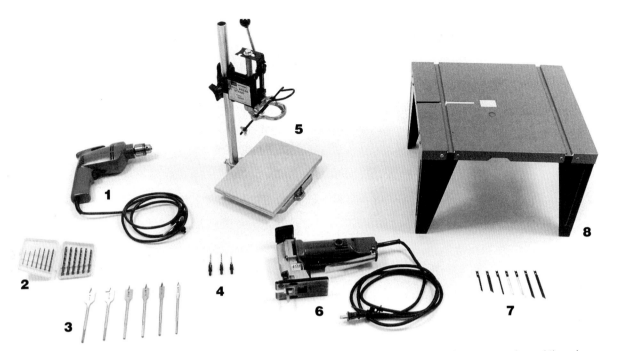

In addition to hand tools, you'll need two inexpensive power tools and accessories for drilling and sawing. The *drilling* tools are (1) an electric drill, (2) speed bits, (3) wood-boring bits, (4) screw drills, and (5) a drill stand. The *sawing* tools are (6) a saber saw, (7) saber saw blades, and (8) a saber saw table.

The drill stand holds the drill vertically and plunges it down toward a worktable when you pull a lever. This makes it easy to drill accurate holes.

A saber saw table holds the saw upside down while you cut and shape small parts. These are available mostly through mail-order tool companies. You may also be able to adapt some router tables to hold saber saws.

Useful (but non-essential) tools. In addition to the basic tools, there are a few that are nice to have. However, you don't absolutely need them unless specified in the instructions. These are:

Miter box (to help make accurate cuts)
Backsaw (to use in the miter box)
Carving (or bench) knives (for shaping parts)
Bench plane (for smoothing wood, truing joints)
Belt sander (for rough sanding and shaping)
Pad sander (for finish-sanding)
Bar clamps (to assemble large projects)

Lumber and Materials

Lumber. Many country woodworking projects require a particular type of wood, or wood planed to several different thicknesses. You can purchase this lumber and have it planed at any lumberyard that specializes in hardwoods. To find the hardwood lumberyards in your area, look in the Yellow Pages under "Lumber — Retail."

Avoid using the construction-grade pine and fir (#2 and #3) sold by lumberyards that cater to builders

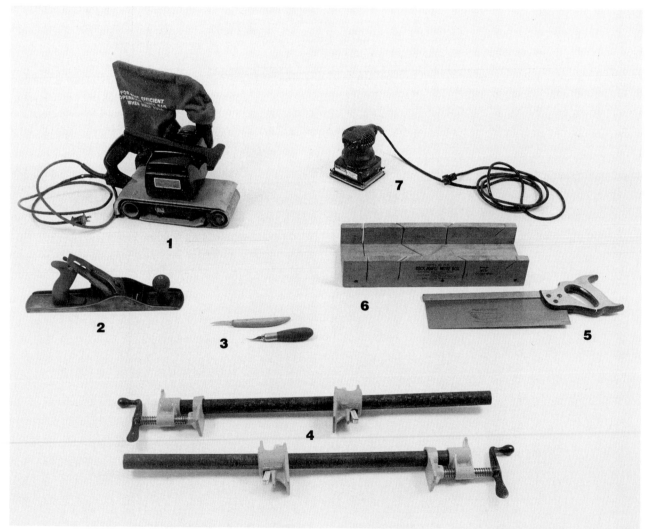

In addition to the tools you *must* have, there are some that are just *nice* to have. These are (1) a belt sander, (2) a bench plane, (3) carving knives, (4) bar clamps, (5) a backsaw, (6) a miter box, and (7) a pad sander.

and carpenters. Even though these yards may carry the correct sizes of lumber — or be willing to cut and plane it for you — construction lumber is not properly dried and seasoned for small woodworking projects. It may begin to warp, split, or crack several months after you finish a project. Before you resort to construction lumber, consider buying your wood through one of the mail-order wood suppliers listed in Appendix B.

If you must use construction-grade lumber, stack it flat in your garage or shop area for three to six months before using it. This will give it a chance to become accustomed to the temperature and humidity indoors. Discard the boards that warp or split, and use only those that remain straight.

Hardware. Most of the hardware required for the projects in this book is sold at local hardware stores or lumberyards. For some special hardware and wooden parts, such as wheels or beads, you may have to visit a crafts or hobby store. If the parts aren't available in either of these locations, contact one of the mail-order suppliers listed in Appendix B.

Many lumberyards offer milling services. They will cut, plane, join, and sometimes even shape lumber for you for a small fee.

You always use the backsaw and the miter box together. These two tools help you make perfect cuts at several angles — 90°, 45° left, and 45° right.

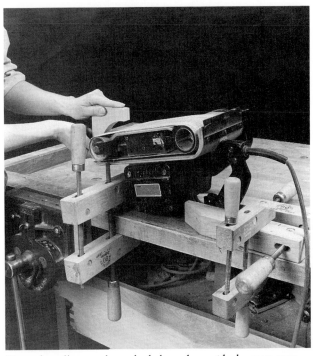

To sand small parts, clamp the belt sander upside down on your workbench. Be very careful not to pinch your fingers between the moving belt and the tool housing.

Plans and Patterns

Plans. Once you have gathered the necessary tools and materials needed for a project, then you must follow the plans. This is not difficult; it's akin to reading a road map. Woodworking plans are commonly written in a standard *orthographic language*. This language consists of lines and symbols that represent the parts of the completed project. The symbols are not hard to decipher; you can figure out most of them with a little common sense. For instance, DIA stands for diameter. CL means centerline. TYP is typical, and so on.

Patterns. Sometimes there are parts of projects that can't be adequately described by the dimensions and symbols on a plan. These odd-shaped parts require patterns. Wherever we could, we've printed patterns full-size. However, some we had to make smaller because they were too big to publish otherwise. We've drawn these scaled-down patterns on a *scale grid* to help you enlarge them.

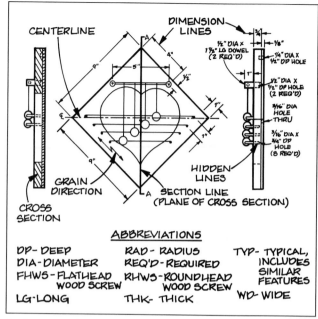

A plan is a road map to your project. As different symbols stand for different geographical features on a map, symbols represent the various parts of a project on a plan.

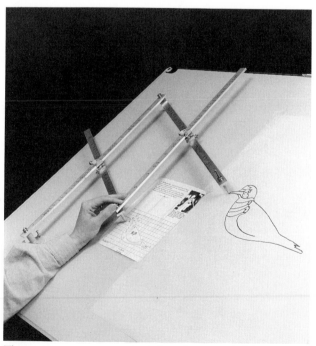

There are two common methods for enlarging scaled-down patterns. Perhaps the easiest is to use a *pantograph*. The simple drawing machines are available at most art and drafting supply stores.

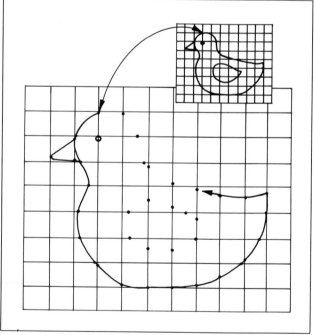

The least expensive is the *squares* method. Draw a full-size grid on a piece of paper. (If the pattern says "1 square = ½"," make the squares on the full-size grid ½" high and ½" wide.) Wherever an object line meets a grid line on the scaled-down pattern, mark a dot on the full-size grid. Then simply connect the dots.

Woodworking Tips and Techniques

Most of the techniques used in *Country Woodworking* are simple and straightforward, just like the projects themselves. Any special techniques that pertain to individual projects are illustrated in the instructions. However, here are a few tips to help with general woodworking:

❖ Sawing

To help make straight, square cuts with a handsaw, clamp a block of scrap wood to the board, flush with the cut line. Use this scrap to guide the saw.

Cut curved shapes with a saber saw or coping saw. Remember, the tighter the curves, the smaller the blade you should use. If you attempt to turn a tight curve with a large blade, the blade may snap.

To cut very tight curves or the bottoms of deep, narrow notches, "nibble" the wood away with the saw blade. Instead of trying to cut along a line, turn the wood so the line is 90° from the saw. Cut up almost to the line, then use the teeth of the saw like a tiny file or rasp to remove the waste.

Use a coping saw to cut dowels and very small wooden parts. When the piece of wood is too small, you can't get a smooth cut with a handsaw or a saber saw.

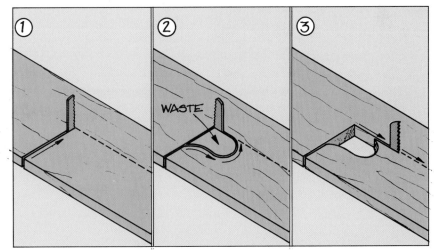

Cut an inside corner with the saber saw in three steps: (1) Cut along one of the pattern lines leading to the corner. (2) When you reach the corner, back up an inch or so and cut a wide arc to the other pattern line. Saw to the corner. (3) Discard the waste, turn the saw around, and continue sawing along the second pattern line, away from the corner.

❖ Drilling

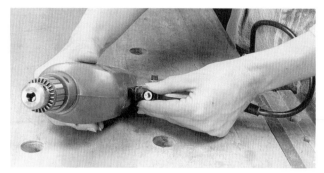

Always drill wood at a slow-to-medium speed — you'll get a smoother hole. Most electric drills have variable speed controls. Some have knobs on the trigger to set the speed.

Use a screw drill to make pilot holes for flathead wood screws. These special drills put a funnel-shaped *countersink* in the wood, so the screw head will rest flush with or slightly below the surface of the wood.

❖ Assembly

Always sand the parts of a project *before* you assemble them — it's much harder to sand them afterward. As you sand each board, be careful not to round over the edges and ends that will join to other boards. A chalk eraser makes a good sanding block.

When you glue wooden parts together, clamp them until the glue dries. Wood glue will not set properly if it doesn't dry under pressure. Wipe away any glue that squeezes out of the joints with a wet (not just damp — wet!) rag.

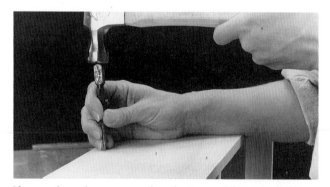

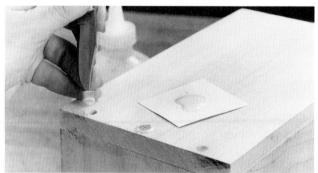

If you nail wooden parts together, don't pound the nails all the way in with a hammer. Stop when they're about 1/16" above the wood, then drive them the rest of the way with a nail punch. This is called *setting* the nails — it prevents you from accidentally hitting the wood with the hammer.

To hide a screw head, drill the countersink about 1/4" below the surface of the wood, making a *counterbore*. Drive the screw, setting the head below the surface. Cut a small length of wooden dowel to make a plug, and glue it in the counterbore. When the glue dries, sand or file the plug flush with the wood surface.

❖ Sanding and Shaping

After the glue dries, some of the wood surfaces may not be aligned as precisely as you'd like. This is normal — wood often shifts slightly as the glue dries. To correct this, sand or file the joints smooth.

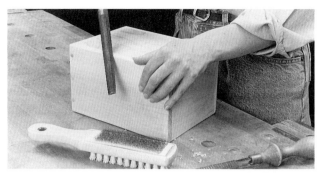

To make the finished project look old and worn, round the corners and edges with a rasp and a file.

Paints and Finishes

Paint. You'll probably want to paint most country woodworking projects after assembling them. Antique country pieces were often painted with colors called *polychromes*. These, however, are no longer available. After experimenting with different types of contemporary paint, we've found that *acrylics* come closest to reproducing the look of polychromes. They also offer other advantages: They're available in a wide range of colors, they can be thinned and cleaned up with water, and they're weatherproof after they dry. Furthermore, you can apply some clear, protective finishes directly over them after they've dried — varnish, polyurethane, tung oil, and Danish oil.

Acrylics come in both tubes and bottles. If you buy the tubes, you may have to mix two or more colors to get some of the hues and tones shown in this book. The bottled paint comes ready-mixed in a huge assortment of colors. You can still mix the bottled paint, if you want, to produce even more colors. We've used a brand called Country Colors because it offers the largest possible assortment and it's available in most craft and hobby stores. The patterns for the projects are color-keyed to the names of the different Country Colors. If you want to mix your own colors from tubes, or use another type of paint, consult the color chart in the Appendix.

When painting a project with acrylics, don't prime the wood or attempt to cover one color with another. Acrylics cover best when they're applied to raw wood. They can be applied over each other when necessary, but it may take several coats to get an even color.

To keep from getting acrylic paint on one part of a project while painting another, cover the area you don't want to paint with masking tape.

Stencils. Many of the painted designs on the *Country Woodworking* projects are easiest to apply with stencils. You can make your own stencils from Mylar™, a stiff, plastic film. You can purchase this film at most art and drafting supply stores. Acrylic paint works well for stenciling, both as the background and as the design. You may need special brushes, however. Buy several sizes, all with stiff bristles.

To make a stencil, first enlarge or copy the pattern onto a piece of paper. Lay transparent plastic film over the paper, and cut the pattern in the plastic with a sharp knife or razor blade.

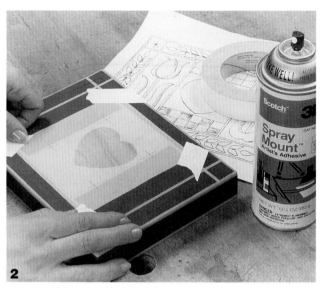

Tape the stencil to the project, carefully positioning the pattern. You may want to apply a spray adhesive to the back side of the stencil so that it lays perfectly flat on the wood surface.

Dip the brush in the paint, *then wipe off most of the paint*. This is very important! You must apply the paint with a brush that is almost dry. If you brush on too much paint at a time, it will bleed underneath the stencil and the edges of the design will be ragged. Apply several thin coats to build up the color.

After applying the paint (and while it's still slightly wet), carefully peel off the stencil. You may have to touch up parts of the design with a fine brush.

COUNTRY WOODWORKING:
A PRIMER

Stains and Finishes. When you want a project to look old, dull the color slightly. To do this, rub a light-colored oil stain over the painted surfaces, then wipe it off before it dries. You may have to experiment with different colors of stain until you get the effect you want.

Another way to achieve an aged look is to sand away small areas of the paint, exposing the wood beneath. Choose these areas carefully, anticipating where the project would get the most wear and tear. Usually, these areas will be along the edges and corners, around handles and knobs, wherever the object will be handled. Stain the exposed wood *slightly* darker. Wood darkens over time when it's exposed to the light.

To protect the painted surface and keep it from becoming worn and dirty, you can apply some clear finishes over the paint. One of the best protective coatings we've found — and the easiest to apply — is a mixture of spar varnish and tung oil. Mix them in equal amounts and apply them with a clean rag, wiping away any excess. Rub on several coats, letting each dry thoroughly. Then buff the finish with #0000 steel wool and paste wax.

To make the finish on a project look old and worn, sand the paint off the areas that will receive the most handling. Stain the exposed wood, making it slightly darker.

Warning: *Don't* apply shellac, lacquer, or alcohol-based stains or finishes over acrylic paint. These dissolve the acrylics.

WATERMELON MAN WHIRLIGIG

n the frontier and in rural settlements, the Sabbath was strictly observed by both adults *and* children. Just as the grown-ups abstained from physical labor, youngsters were expected to refrain from boisterous activity. To keep the children occupied during the hours that they weren't in church, they were given playthings that were especially designed to encourage quiet play, yet still appeal to their whimsy and imagination. Whirligigs were the perfect such "Sunday toys." They required no physical participation — just watch the wind blow the figures 'round and 'round.

This particular whirligig is copied from a famous antique toy, now in the collection of the Museum of American Folk Art, New York City. A farmer with his arms outstretched twirls slices of watermelon. While he performs this fanciful juggling act, an arrow, or "wind vane," keeps him pointed into the wind. This wind vane pivots on a metal rod.

Special Tools

A hacksaw, to cut the metal parts

Shopping List

¾"-thick stock (a 1 x 12, at least
    20" long)
¼"-thick stock (a small scrap, about
4" x 5")
¾"-diameter dowel, at least 12" long
⅛"-diameter dowel, at least 2" long
¼"-diameter metal rod, at least
    4" long
³⁄₁₆"-diameter metal rod, at least
    11¾" long
#10 x 2" flathead wood screws (2)
16d common nail (just 1)
Epoxy glue
Medium and fine sandpaper
Paint

**EXPLODED
VIEW**

CUTTING LIST

Wooden Parts

A. Farmer's
   body   ¾" x 4⅛" x 13¼"
B. Farmer's
   arms (2)   ¾" diameter x 4"
C. Farmer's
   hands (2)   ¾" diameter x ¾"
D. Pegs (2)   ⅛" diameter x ¾"
E. Watermelon
   slices (2)   ¼" x 1½" x 3¾"
F. Wind vane   ¾" x 3½" x 18"
G. Base   5" diameter x ¾"

Metal Parts

H. Axle   ³⁄₁₆" diameter x 11¾"
J. Pivot   ¼" diameter x 4"

1. Carefully select your materials. Before you purchase the materials for this project, decide where you will use it. If you intend to place the whirligig outside, use either mahogany or poplar to make the wooden parts. These woods last much longer out-of-doors than other species. You can find either wood at any lumberyard that sells hardwoods.

To bond the parts of an outdoor whirligig together, use a waterproof glue such as epoxy or resorcinol. Both of these are available at hardware stores.

If the whirligig will only be displayed indoors, make it from any soft or medium-hard wood, such as white pine or poplar. Glue the parts together with carpenter's (yellow) glue.

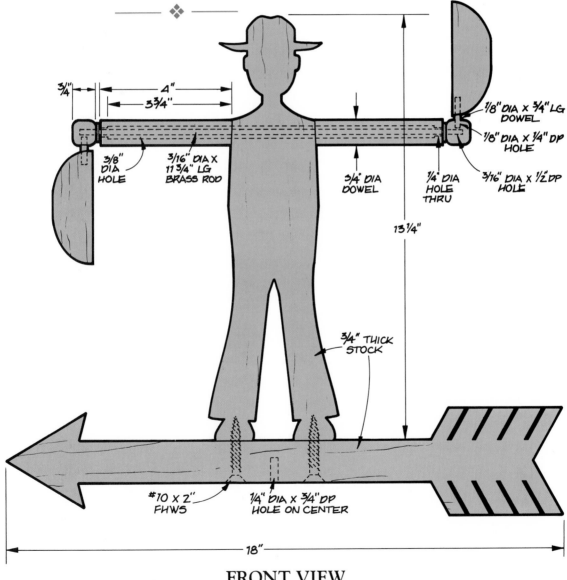

FRONT VIEW

Figure 1. To drill the holes in the arms exactly 3¾" deep, wrap a piece of tape around the drill bit 3¾" from the end. Stop drilling when the tape reaches the wood.

2. Cut the wooden and metal parts to size. This project is made mostly from wood, with a little bit of metal rod. The metal is used for the moving parts. This helps the whirligig to last longer. If you were to make the moving parts from wood, they would quickly wear out.

Use an ordinary saw to cut the wooden parts, and a hacksaw to cut the metal parts. Make all of the pieces — both wood and metal — the sizes shown in the Cutting List. Using a file, remove any burrs from the cut ends of the metal parts.

3. Cut the shapes of the wooden parts. Enlarge the patterns for the body, the watermelon slices, and the wind vane. Trace these onto the stock, then cut out the shapes with a saber saw. Sand the sawed edges to remove the saw marks.

4. Drill the axle holes. The watermelon slices are actually the blades of a rotor that turns on an axle as the wind blows. This axle passes through the body and the arms of the whirligig, as shown in the Front View. To make the holes for this axle, drill ⅜"-diameter holes through the body, and 3¾" into the length of each arm from one end. (See Figure 1.)

Turn each arm around, and drill a ¼"-diameter hole in the other end until it meets with the ⅜"-diameter hole you just drilled. The Axle Hole Cutaway drawing shows how these two holes should intersect. The reason for using two different hole diameters for the axle hole is to reduce the friction. The axle rubs the wood only at the ends of the arms where you have drilled the ¼"-diameter holes. Along most of its length — as the axle passes through the ⅜"-diameter holes — it doesn't touch the wood at all. This, in turn, helps the whirligig turn more freely.

❖

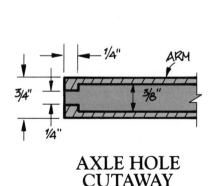

**AXLE HOLE
CUTAWAY**

WATERMELON MAN
WHIRLIGIG

WATER-MELON WIND PADDLE

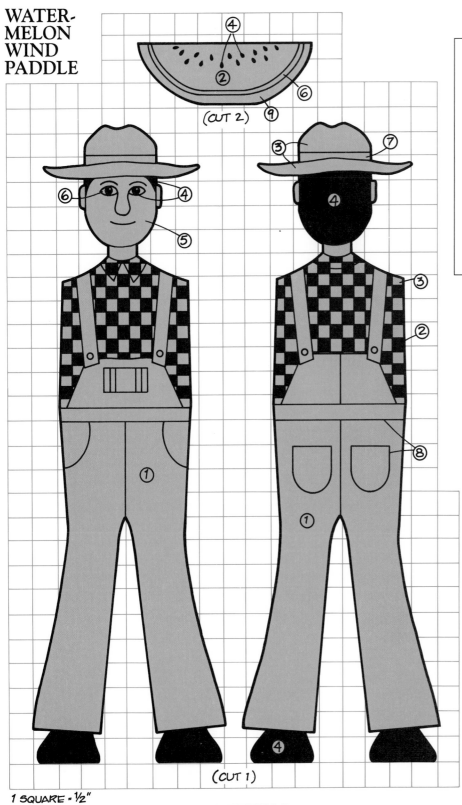

(CUT 2)

(CUT 1)

1 SQUARE = ½"

BODY PATTERN

Figure 2. Using the file, create a small flat area on each end of the axle. When you attach the hands, the glue will fill the flat and help keep the hands from turning on the axle.

5. Drill the remaining holes. The remaining holes in the wooden parts are straightforward and much simpler to make. All but the pilot holes for the screws are "stopped" — that is, they don't go completely through the wood. Use a piece of tape around your drill bit (as in the last step) to help judge the depth of each hole. Here's a list of the holes you need to make:

- ¼"-diameter x ½"-deep hole in the center of the base to hold the pivot
- ¼"-diameter x ¾"-deep hole in the shaft of the wind vane to make a "cup" for the pivot
- ³⁄₁₆"-diameter x ½"-deep holes in one end of each hand to attach them to the axle
- ⅛"-diameter x ¼"-deep holes in each hand to attach the watermelon slices
- ⅛"-diameter x ½"-deep holes in each watermelon slice to attach them to the hands

Also drill pilot holes for the screws that will hold the farmer to the wind vane. Use a screw drill bit to make these holes, as discussed on page 14 in the Introduction. Countersink the holes so that the heads of the flathead screws will rest flush with the surface of the wood.

6. Assemble the parts of the farmer. Using epoxy glue, attach the arms to the body. To make sure that the arms stand out straight from the body, put the axle in place while the glue cures. Take care that you don't get any glue on the axle!

After the glue joint between the body and the arms hardens, attach the hands to the ends of the axles. To make sure that the hands don't slip on the axle, file a small flat area, on each end of the axle. (See Figure 2.) Place two or three drops of epoxy glue in the ³⁄₁₆"-diameter holes in the ends of the hands, then press the hands onto the axle.

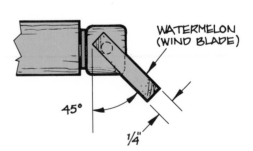

WIND BLADE DETAIL

Before the glue joint between the hands and the axle sets, attach the watermelon slices to the hands with glue and pegs. Position the hands so that one watermelon slice points up and the other points down. Then angle the slices, as shown in the Wind Blade Detail drawing, so that one slice is angled to the *right* and the other is angled to the *left*, as you look at the top of the farmer. Let the glue dry completely.

———— ❖ ————

7. File a point on the pivot. While the glue is drying on the farmer, grind a point on one end of the pivot. This point will reduce the friction of the pivot, and help the wind vane to turn easier. To make the point, first clamp the file to your workbench. Then secure the metal pivot in the drill chuck as if it were a drill bit. Turn the drill on, and hold the end of the pivot against the file at a slight angle. The file will slowly grind a point on the pivot. (See Figure 3.)

———— ❖ ————

8. Assemble the parts of the wind vane. Put a few drops of epoxy glue into the ¼"-diameter hole in the base, then press the blunt end of the pivot into the hole. Using the hacksaw, cut the head off a 16d nail. Put a few drops of glue in the ¼"-diameter hole in the wind vane, then drop the nail head in the hole. Tamp it flat in the bottom of the hole with the shaft of the nail.

Mount the wind vane on the pivot. The pointed end of the pivot should rest against the head of the nail. (Without the nail head, the pivot would eventually bite through the wooden wind vane.) The wind vane should rotate freely on the pivot. If it binds, apply a little furniture wax to the inside of the pivot hole.

———— ❖ ————

Figure 3. Use an electric drill and a file to grind a point on the pivot. Work slowly, and don't press the pivot too hard against the file. If you press too hard, you won't be able to hold the pivot steady on the file. It will try to wander off.

Colors Shown:
① HARVEST GOLD

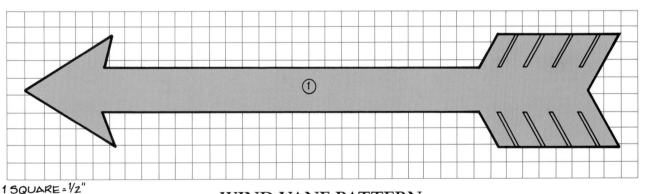

1 SQUARE = ½"

WIND VANE PATTERN

9. Attach the farmer to the wind vane. When you're satisfied that the wind vane works properly, and that the watermelon slices revolve freely, attach the farmer to the wind vane. Drive screws up through the shaft of the wind vane and into the feet of the farmer. Don't glue these assemblies together. Just attach them with screws, so that you can take them apart easily if you need to repair them or touch up the paint.

10. Finish-sand the completed whirligig. Disassemble the wind vane from the base, and remove the farmer from the wind vane. Using medium-grit sandpaper, round over the edges of the farmer and the wind vane to make them look worn. Switch to fine grit, smoothing the entire surface of the project.

11. Paint the completed whirligig. Trace the features of the farmer and the watermelon slices onto the wood. Then carefully paint the project. If you intend to use the whirligig outside, use exterior paints. After the paint dries, reassemble the farmer, wind vane, and base.

SIX-BOARD BENCH

Country craftsmen made many pieces of furniture for expediency. The six-board bench is a good example. Just nail together six boards and presto! Instant seating.

However, just because a piece is easy to build doesn't mean that it isn't well made. Not only is this bench an example of expedient woodworking, it shows practical and economical craftsmanship. Although there are only six boards, they are cleverly arranged to brace each other. This keeps the bench stable and solid. There are many eighteenth- and nineteenth-century benches that are still serviceable today.

A simple project can also be well designed. The fretwork aprons soften the no-nonsense design, and make it pleasing to the eye. It's this blend of utility and imagination that makes the six-board bench a classic example of country furniture design.

EXPLODED VIEW

Special Tools

Bar clamps (not necessary, but very helpful)

Shopping List

¾"-thick stock (a 1 x 12, at least 96" long)

#10 x 1¼" flathead wood screws (20–24)

⅜"-diameter dowel (about 12" long)

Paint, stain, or finish

Carpenter's (yellow) glue or resorcinol

CUTTING LIST

A.	Top	¾" x 11¼" x 29"
B.	Legs (2)	¾" x 8¾" x 16¼"
C.	Aprons (2)	¾" x 2¾" x 26½"
D.	Stretcher	¾" x 1½" x 22½"

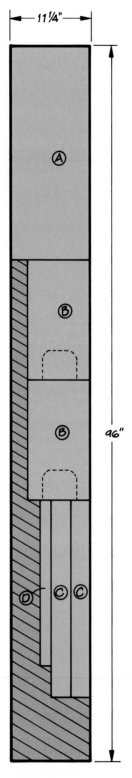

CUTTING DIAGRAM

1. Choose the materials. Most country benches were made from lightweight, durable woods, such as white or yellow pine, to make them easy to move without sacrificing sturdiness. This particular bench is designed to be made from ordinary 1 x 12 pine stock, which can be bought at any lumberyard.

❖

2. Cut and shape the parts. Cut the parts to the sizes in the Cutting List. The Cutting Diagram shows you how to get all six parts out of a single 8'-long 1 x 12.

Enlarge the Apron Pattern and trace it on the stock. Also lay out the cutout at the bottom of each leg, as shown in the Side View. Cut the shapes of the aprons and legs, using a saber saw or a coping saw. Sand the sawed edges smooth.

❖

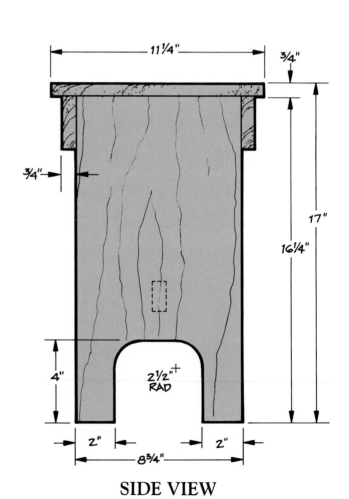

SIDE VIEW

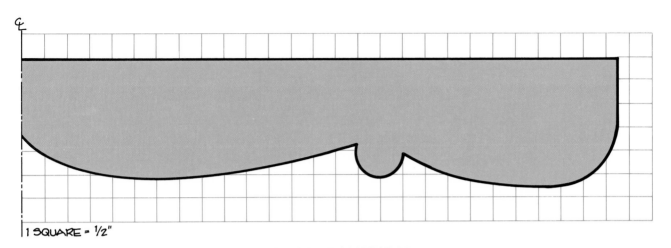

APRON PATTERN
(HALF SIZE)

1 SQUARE = 1/2"

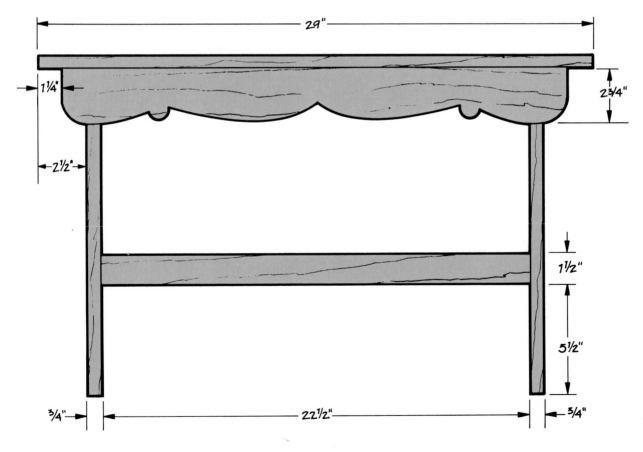

FRONT VIEW

Figure 1. To hide the screw heads, glue dowel plugs in the counterbores. After the glue dries, sand or file the plugs flush with the wooden surface.

3. Assemble the bench. Finish-sand the faces of all the parts. Glue the aprons to the legs, attach the stretcher between the legs, then join the top to the legs and the aprons. Reinforce all joints with screws.

Use the screw drill to counterbore and countersink the screw heads. The counterbores should be about ¼" deep, so the heads will rest below the surface. With a coping saw, cut the ⅜"-diameter dowel into ⅜"-long plugs. Dip these plugs in glue and press them into the counterbores, covering the screw heads. (See Figure 1.)

With a wet rag, wipe off any glue that squeezes out of the joints or from around the plugs. Let the remaining glue dry. File and sand the plugs even with the wood surface, as shown in the Screw Joinery Detail.

Note: If you plan to use the bench outside, assemble the parts with resorcinol glue. This waterproof glue is made especially for kitchen, bath, and outdoor woodworking projects. It comes in two parts — resin and activator — and must be mixed before you use it. It's available at most hardware stores and lumberyards.

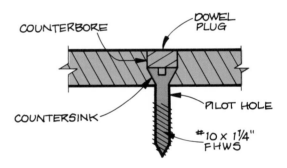

SCREW JOINERY DETAIL

4. Paint or finish the bench. Lightly sand the entire bench to clean the surfaces, then paint it or finish it. Traditionally, country craftsmen painted their benches with milk paint. Several companies still make old-time milk paint, and it is available at most paint stores and arts and crafts supply centers. If you will be using the bench outdoors, paint it with exterior latex paint, then apply a coat of linseed oil. This creates a look that is very similar to milk paint.

If you don't paint the bench, stain it and cover it with a clear, durable finish. For outdoor benches, use spar varnish over an oil-based stain.

COUNTRY TRASH CAN

he difficulty with country decor is that some modern essentials just don't fit. For instance, if you "countrify" your kitchen, how do you deal with the trash can? Contemporary trash containers are invariably made of plastic, which looks decidedly uncountry.

One way around this dilemma is to disguise the container — hide it inside something that *is* country. Most old-time kitchens and pantries had storage bins for fruits and vegetables that were about the same size as a modern trash can. With a little ingenuity, you can build a hollow wooden bin that will hold a plastic trash container.

The storage bin shown holds a standard 20-gallon plastic trash can. The wooden lid is hinged to the top, so the plastic can remains hidden except when the lid is lifted to throw away some garbage. When you need to empty or clean the trash can, remove the wooden top by loosening two hook-and-eye catches.

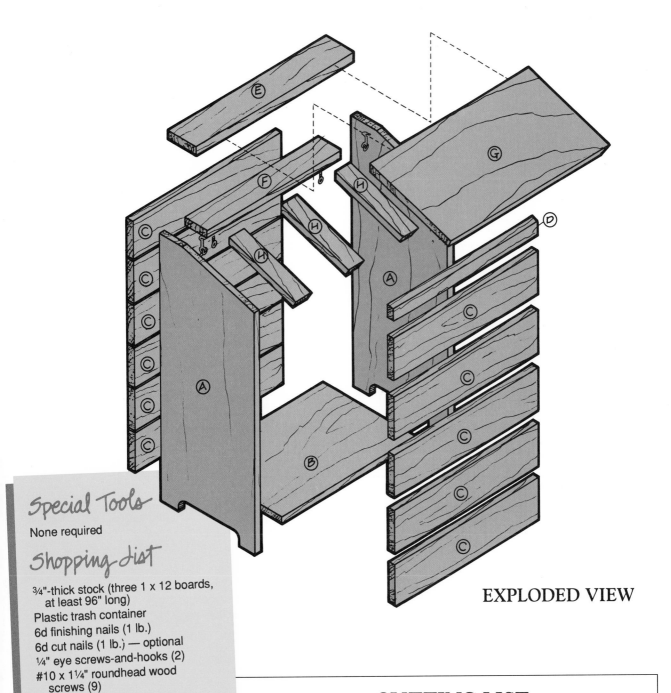

EXPLODED VIEW

CUTTING LIST

A.	Sides (2)	¾" x 11¼" x 28¼"	E.	Top	¾" x 3¾" x 19½"
B.	Bottom	¾" x 11¼" x 16½"	F.	Top brace	¾" x 2⅞" x 16⅜"
C.	Front/back slats (11)	¾" x 4¼" x 18"	G.	Lid	¾" x 11" x 19½"
D.	Top front slat	¾" x 1" x 18"	H.	Lid braces (3)	¾" x 2" x 8¼"

1. Choose the materials. Most country storage bins of this type were made from inexpensive, easy-to-work wood, such as white pine or poplar. We built the bin shown from yellow pine. All of these are good choices. You can also use old, weathered barn wood, if you are lucky enough to find some.

When shopping for a plastic trash container, look for one approximately the same size as the bin. The trash bin shown was designed for a Rubbermaid™ 20-gallon trash container. If you purchase another brand, you may have to change the dimensions of the bin slightly.

2. Cut the parts to size. Cut the ¾"-thick stock to the sizes shown in the Cutting List. Bevel-cut the adjoining edges of the top and lid at 7½°, as shown in the Lid/Top Layout. Also bevel-cut the top edge of the top front slat and the back ends of the lid braces at 15°.

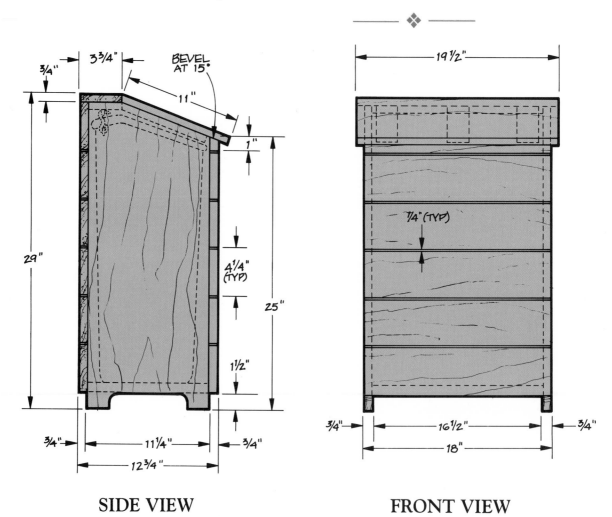

SIDE VIEW   **FRONT VIEW**

3. Cut the shape of the sides. Mark the shape of the sides on the stock, as shown in the Side Layout. Miter the top edge and cut the shape of the feet with a saber saw. Sand the edges to remove the saw marks.

———— ❖ ————

4. Assemble the bin. Finish-sand all the parts you have made, then assemble them with glue and finishing nails. First, attach the sides to the bottom, making sure the bottom is flush with the leg cutout on the sides. Then attach the front and back slats. Leave a ¼" gap between each slat. These gaps let the slats expand and contract. They also help ventilate the bin, preventing humidity from building up inside.

As you work, use a wet rag to wipe away any glue that squeezes out of the joints. Also, set the head of the nails slightly below the surface of the wood with a nail punch. When the glue dries, sand all the joints clean and, wherever necessary, the surfaces flush.

———— ❖ ————

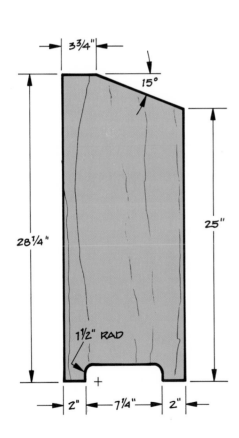

SIDE LAYOUT

Tip: If you wish to make the project look more authentic, use cut nails *instead of finishing nails to assemble the trash bin. These square-shank nails imitate the look of hand-forged nails — the only nails available to most early nineteenth-century country craftsmen.*

To drive a cut nail, first drill a ³/16"-diameter pilot hole. (If you don't drill this hole, the nail will split the wood.) Place tip of the nail in the hole and pound it into the wood with a hammer. (See Figure 1.) There's no need to set the head.

Figure 1. To drive a cut nail, first drill a pilot hole, then pound it into the wood. These square-shank nails imitate the look of the old-time cut nails that were used to assemble early country furniture pieces.

— ❖ —

5. Attach the top and lid. Both the top and the lid must be braced, but for different reasons. The braces on the lid keep the part from warping, while the brace on the top serves as a plug. To attach the brace to the top, simply glue the parts together, positioning the brace as shown in the Lid/Top Layout.

— ❖ —

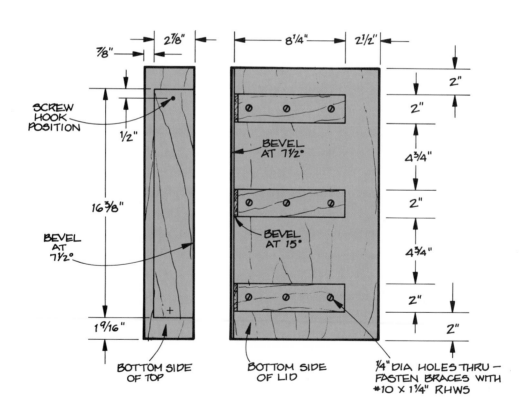

LID/TOP LAYOUT

Attaching the braces to the lid is a bit more involved. As mentioned before, the lid must be braced so it doesn't cup or warp. At the same time, it must be allowed to expand and contract with changes in temperature and humidity. If you simply nail or glue braces to the underside of the lid, the results will be worse than if you had used no braces at all. The lid may begin to warp and split almost immediately.

To brace the lid *and* allow for the natural movement of the wood, attach the braces with screws in oversize holes. Drill ¼"-diameter pilot holes through the braces, and ⅛"-diameter pilot holes in the lid. Place flat washers on #10 x 1¼" roundhead wood screws, then drive them through the braces and into the doors. Tighten the screws so they're snug, but not so tight that the washers bite into the wood.

Although the screws are held firmly in the lid, they're loose in the brace. (The screw shanks are slightly smaller than the ¼"-diameter holes.) This gives the lid the freedom to shrink and swell slightly, sliding over the braces. Yet the lid is still held snug against the braces and remains flat. (See Figure 2.)

The top and the lid attach to the bin with hooks and eyes. This makes it easy to remove the top/lid assembly when you need to empty or clean the plastic trash container. To install these hooks and eyes, first drive the hooks into the underside of the top brace. Put the top on the bin, letting the hooks dangle down. Mark the inside of the bin where the points of the hooks touch. Remove the top and install eye screws at the marks.

Replace the top and secure the hooks in the eyes. They should hold the top snug, but not so snug that it's difficult to latch and unlatch the hooks. If the top is too tight or too loose, remove the eyes and move them up or down slightly.

When the hooks-and-eyes are installed, secure the top to the bin. Put the lid in place, butting the lid's beveled edge up against the beveled edge of the top. Position the strap hinges to straddle the parts and mark the location of the mounting screws. Remove the hinges, drill ⅛"-diameter pilot holes, then attach the hinges to the top and lid.

Figure 2. Drill oversize pilot holes in the lid braces to allow the lid to expand and contract with changes in the weather.

6. Paint or finish the trash bin. Remove the top/lid assembly from the bin, then remove all the hardware from the top, lid, and bin. Set the hardware aside and lightly sand the wooden surfaces clean.

Stain, finish, or paint the bin. (The bin shown is stained and finished with polyurethane.) Carefully apply as many coats of paint or finish to the inside surface of the bin as you do to the outside. This will help keep the finished piece from splitting or distorting over time.

When the paint or finish dries, replace the hardware. Place the plastic trash container in the bin, then secure the top and lid.

TULIP BOX

ong before there were year-round florists or artificial flowers, folks longed for a little touch of spring in the dead of winter. One way to soothe this longing was with a wooden tulip box. The box was placed on the windowsill, where the sunlight would play across the brightly colored heads of the tulips, relieving the dreary grayish-white of winter.

Some folks saw a good deal more than bright colors in these wooden flower boxes. Tulips were a potent symbol among the Pennsylvania Dutch. Three-petal tulips reminded them of the Trinity — Father, Son, and Holy Ghost. Tulip boxes often held three tulips, the middle tulip slightly higher than the other two. This was another symbol: Jesus on the cross between the two thieves.

Whatever comfort the maker derived from his box — whether it was the dance of light and color or the promise of spiritual resurrection — the box often stayed on the sill until spring, when it could finally be replaced by the real thing.

EXPLODED VIEW

CUTTING LIST

A.	Box sides (2)	¾" x 3½" x 14½"	G.	Middle leaves	¾" x 8½" x 10"	
B.	Box ends (2)	¾" x 3½" x 2¾"	H.	Right leaves	¾" x 7¼" x 7½"	
C.	Base/ bottom (2)	¾" x 2¾" x 13"	J.	Left stem	¼"-diameter x 9½"	
D.	Spacers (2)	¾" x 1" x 2¾"	K.	Middle stem	¼"-diameter x 11¾"	
E.	Tulip heads (3)	¾" x 3½" x 3½"	L.	Right stem	¼"-diameter x 10¼"	
F.	Left leaves	¾" x 8" x 8"				

1. Choose the materials. Because of the way wood grain runs through a board, some areas of the leaves will be fragile after they are cut to shape. The tips may break off, or they may split at the base. To make the leaves less vulnerable, select a medium-soft wood, such as yellow pine or poplar, for this project. These woods are easy to cut and shape, yet are relatively strong.

❖

2. Cut the parts to size. Cut all the wooden parts to the sizes specified in the Cutting List. The Cutting Diagram shows how to make all the ¾"-thick parts from a single 1 x 10, 51" long. Cut the stems to size from the same 36"-long dowels. Sand the ends of the stems to remove any splinters.

❖

3. Drill the holes to mount the tulips. Tape the base and the bottom together so that all the edges are flush. Mark the locations of the ¼"-diameter stem holes on the base, as shown in the Base Layout.

Drill through both pieces at the same time, boring down through the base and ½" into the bottom. To gauge the depth of the holes, wrap a piece of tape around the drill bit 1¼" from the end.

Stop drilling just as the tape reaches the surface of the wood. (See Figure 1.)

❖

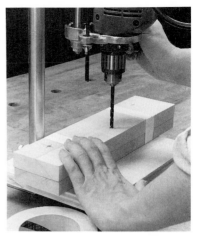

Figure 1. To make sure that the stem holes line up, drill the base and bottom of the box at the same time. This technique is called "pad drilling."

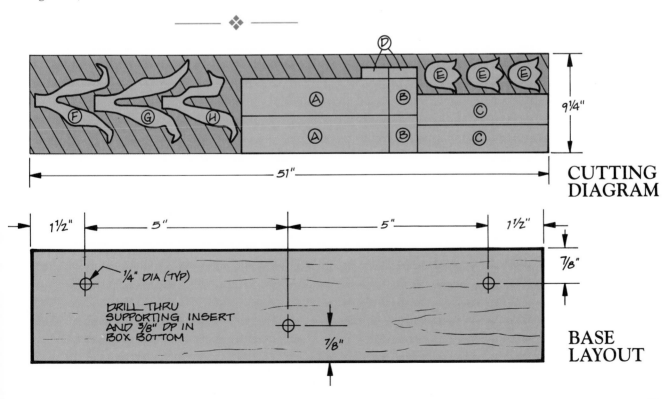

CUTTING DIAGRAM

BASE LAYOUT

¼" DIA (TYP)

DRILL THRU SUPPORTING INSERT AND ⅜" DP IN BOX BOTTOM

4. **Drill the holes in the leaves and the tulips.** It's easier to make the holes in the tulips and leaves *before* you cut them to shape. Enlarge the patterns, and trace them onto the stock. Mark the locations of the ¼"-diameter holes.

Clamp the stock to your workbench and drill each hole. The holes in the base of the flowers are ½" deep. Wrap a piece of tape around the drill bit, as you did in the previous step, so you know when to stop drilling.

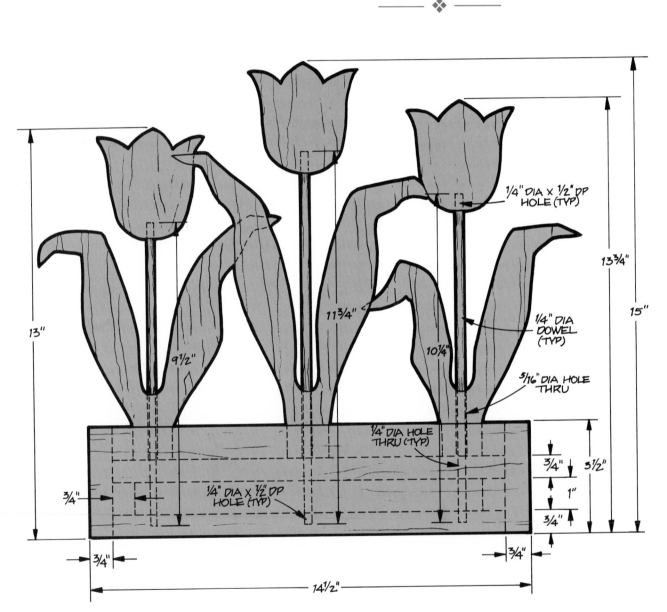

FRONT VIEW

5. Cut the shape of the tulips and leaves. After you make the holes, cut the shapes with a saber saw. Sand the sawed edges to remove the saw marks.

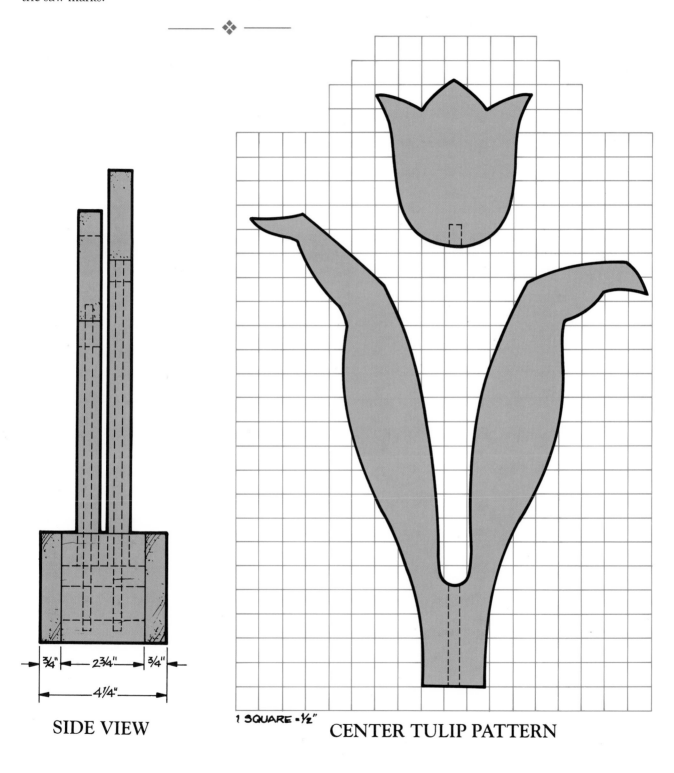

3/4" 2 3/4" 3/4"

4 1/4"

SIDE VIEW

1 SQUARE = 1/2" **CENTER TULIP PATTERN**

Figure 2. Stencil the front and back sides of the box, if you want to add a decoration. Refer to the Introduction for instructions on how to make and apply a stencil.

6. Assemble the box. Finish-sand the parts of the box, except the bottom and the spacers. Apply glue to the edges of the base and face of the spacers, then nail the base and the bottom to the spacers. Pound the nails partway into the stock, then insert the stems in their holes to check that the holes line up.

If the stems are difficult to insert, disassemble the parts before the glue dries. Line up the holes again and put the base, bottom, and spacers back together. When the stems can be inserted easily, drive the nails flush with the surface of the wood.

Spread glue on one end of the base and the bottom, and nail a box end in place. Repeat for the other end.

Spread glue on the front edges of the base, bottom, and ends, and nail the front side in place. Repeat for the back side. Wipe away any excess glue with a damp rag.

— ❖ —

7. Paint the box and the tulips. After the glue dries on the box, sand all the joints to make them clean and flush. Do any touch-up sanding necessary to the tulip flowers, stems, and leaves. Lightly sand the edges of the flowers and leaves to round them over.

Paint the box and the tulips the colors suggested, or use your own color scheme. Stencil the design shown here — or one of your own choosing — to the sides of the box. (See Figure 2.)

— ❖ —

8. Assemble the tulips in the box. Apply a little glue to the upper ends of the stems and the holes in the tulips. Insert the stems in the holes and let the glue dry.

Insert the stems through the holes in the leaves, and mount the assembled tulips in the box. *Don't* glue the leaves to the stems, nor glue the stems in the box. It's easier to dust and clean the box if you can take it apart. You can also change the flowers and the leaves around when you get tired of the arrangement.

— ❖ —

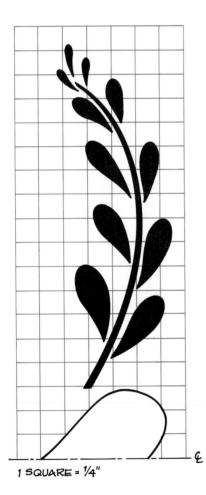

1 SQUARE = ¼"

STENCIL PATTERN

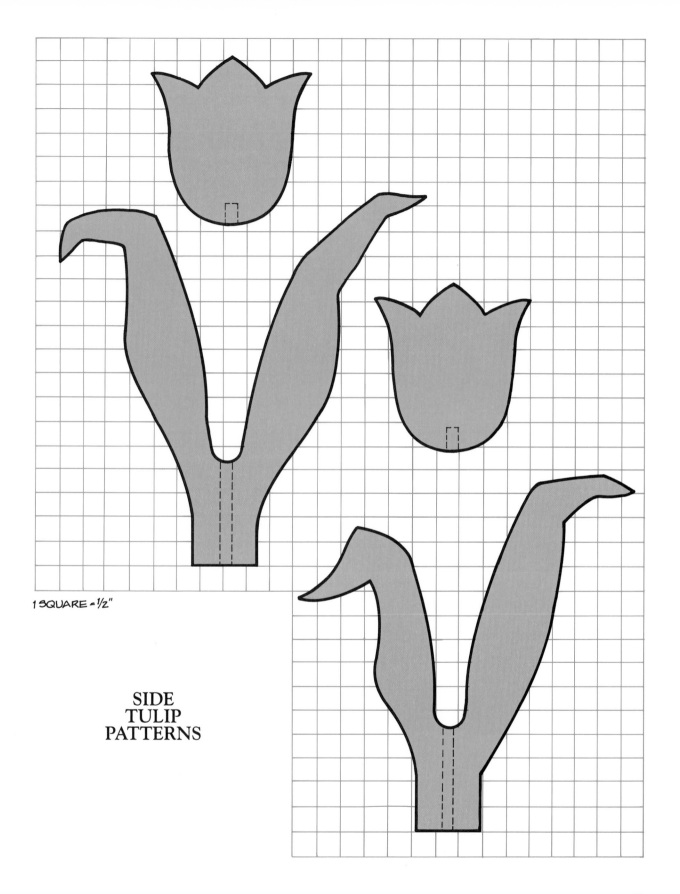

1 SQUARE = 1/2"

SIDE
TULIP
PATTERNS

GAME BARD

Board games were a popular pastime in early American homes. Almost every family had at least one game board, most had several. True to their frugal, space-saving ways, country folk usually made these boards reversible, painting a different game on each side: This checkerboard has a pachisi pattern on the back.

The games they played were much the same as those we play today — chess, checkers, pachisi, and backgammon, for example. There were some subtle differences, however. Checkerboards often had more squares than we use nowadays — as many as twelve to a side. The players used the same number of pieces as we do — twelve apiece — but they arranged the checkers at the beginning of the game with gaps in the ranks. The opponents had more room to maneuver, and this made the game more interesting. These boards were referred to as Canadian checkerboards, since they were most popular in the northern states and in Canada.

The pattern for this game board is a regular American checkerboard, with eight squares to a side. This makes it easier to use, since most of us have been taught to play on a 64-square board. If you'd rather make an old-style Canadian checkerboard with 100 or 144 squares, simply change the spacing on the grid and the diameter of the checkers.

Special Tools

Backsaw, to cut miter joints and small parts
Miter box, to guide the backsaw

Shopping List

¾"-thick plywood (at least 13" square)
¾"-thick stock (at least ¾" wide and 2" long)
½"-thick stock (at least ½" wide and 18" long)
¼"-thick stock (at least 1" wide and 56" long)
1⅜"-diameter closet pole (at least 14" long)
¾" wire brads (16–20)
Carpenter's (yellow) glue
Paint

CUTTING LIST

A. Game board   ¾" x 13" x 13"
B. Edge
    moldings (4)   ¼" x 1" x 13½"
C. Checkers
    (24)   1⅜" diameter x ⅜"
D. Pachisi
    pieces (16)   ½" x ½" x 1"
E. Dice (2)   ¾" x ¾" x ¾"

Figure 1. Most miter boxes have a 90° slot so you can make square cuts as well as angled cuts. This is useful when cutting slender stock to length.

Figure 2. You can use a miter box to cut round as well as rectangular stock. Press the round stock up against one of the walls of the box to hold it steady.

1. Choose the materials. Make the checkerboard from plywood, which is more stable than solid wood and doesn't expand and contract with changes in temperature and humidity. If you use solid wood for the board, it may expand enough to pop the miter joints at the corners — and ruin your project.

Make the remaining parts from solid wood. You may be able to use scraps for all but the checkers. It's easiest to make these from a large dowel or closet pole. Closet pole stock can be purchased from most lumberyards and building supply centers.

---

2. Cut the parts to size. Cut all the parts to the dimensions in the Cutting List. Use the backsaw and miter box to cut the moldings to length, mitering the ends at 45°.

Also use the backsaw and miter box to cut the checkers, pachisi pieces, and dice. (See Figures 1 and 2.) These parts are too small to cut with a handsaw or a saber saw; it's too difficult to grasp them while you cut them. A miter box, however, holds slender stock for you while you slice it with the backsaw.

---

3. Draw the game board patterns. Draw the patterns for the checkerboard and the pachisi board on the plywood *before* you attach the moldings. If you wait until afterward, you'll find it difficult to lay a straightedge against the board because the moldings will get in the way. Enlarge the Pachisi Pattern and trace it on the board. There's no need to enlarge the Checkerboard Layout, since this is just a simple grid. Simply measure it and mark it on the wood.

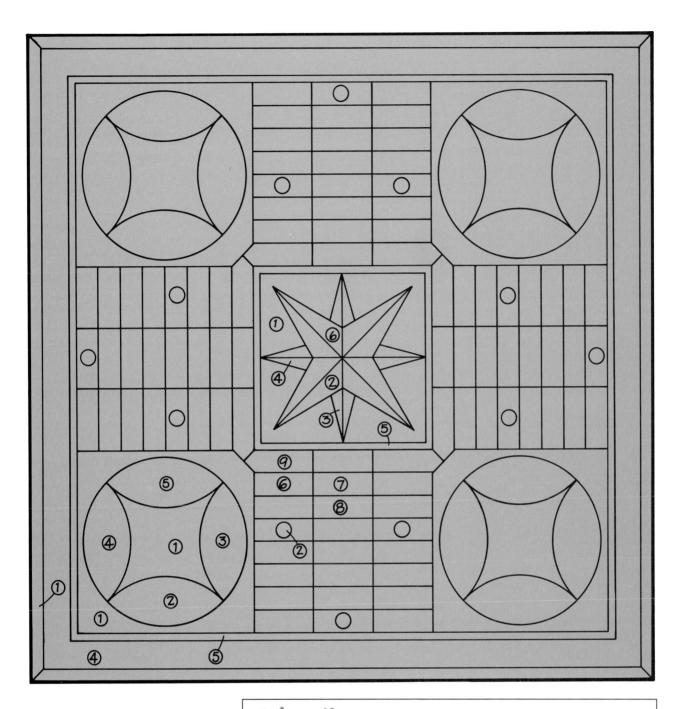

PACHISI PATTERN
(HALF SIZE)

Colors Shown:

1. SOFT BLACK (INCLUDES EDGING)
2. JOSONJA RED
3. CHESAPEAKE BLUE
4. GREEN OLIVE
5. GOLDEN HARVEST

6. EQUAL PARTS OFF WHITE AND GOLDEN HARVEST
7. EQUAL PARTS OFF WHITE AND CHESAPEAKE BLUE
8. TWO PARTS OFF WHITE AND ONE PART CHESAPEAKE BLUE
9. OFF WHITE

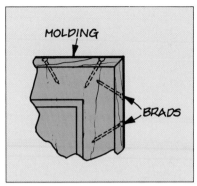

Figure 3. By driving the brads at alternating angles, as shown, you help to anchor the molding to the game board. Even if the glue joint should break, the molding will remain in place.

Figure 4. When sanding small wooden pieces, it's easier to rub them on the sandpaper than to rub the sandpaper on them.

4. Attach the moldings. Finish-sand the faces of the moldings and the plywood. Glue the moldings to the plywood and reinforce the glue joints with ¾" wire brads. Drive the brads at slight angles, changing the angle for each brad. (See Figure 3.) This will help anchor the moldings to the plywood.

With a wet rag, wipe away any glue that squeezes out of the joints. Let the remaining glue dry completely, then sand the miter joints clean and flush. Round the edges of the moldings with sandpaper.

❖

5. Paint the game board and game pieces. Finish-sand all the game pieces. Round the edges of the dice so they tumble properly. The easiest way to sand these small parts is to staple a sheet of sandpaper to a wide, flat wood scrap. Rub the pieces back and forth on the sandpaper. (See Figure 4.)

Paint the game board as suggested, or use your own color scheme. Remember, you need to use two different colors for the checkers (twelve of each), and four different colors for the pachisi pieces (four of each).

If you intend to use the game board, apply a coat of clear varnish or polyurethane over the paint. This will help protect the colors and keep them from getting dirty.

❖

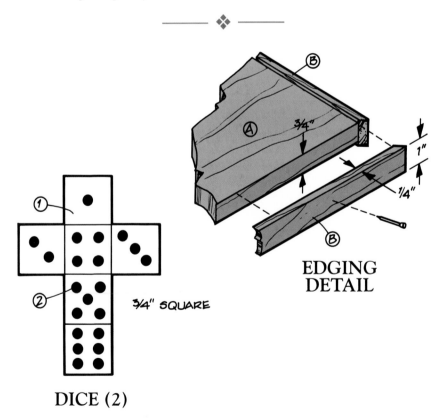

EDGING DETAIL

¾" SQUARE

DICE (2)

Colors Shown:
① GOLDEN HARVEST
② SOFT BLACK

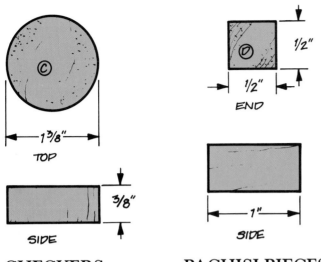

CHECKERS

PACHISI PIECES

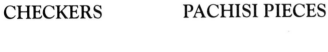

Colors Shown:

CHECKERS

12 — SOFT BLACK
12 — JOSONJA RED

PACHISI PIECES

4 each — GOLDEN HARVEST
CHESAPEAKE BLUE
GREEN OLIVE
JOSONJA RED

CHECKERBOARD

① JOSONJA RED
② SOFT BLACK
③ CHESAPEAKE BLUE

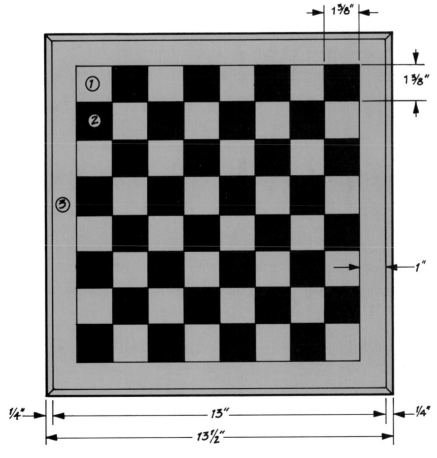

CHECKERBOARD
LAYOUT

ALPHABET BLOCKS

**B**efore the invention of talking computers and similar electronic marvels, children learned their alphabet by playing with blocks. They also learned phonics and basic spelling from those same blocks. These primitive playthings packed a lot of education!

The concept was ingeniously simple. The blocks were brightly colored wooden cubes, which a child could fit together any way he wished. Toymakers painted two sides of each cube with a single letter of the alphabet. They painted another two with simple objects or animals whose names began with the same letter that was painted on an adjacent side. Once the child understood that each letter represented a different sound, he or she arranged the blocks to spell words. This is the same reasoning process needed to use a talking computer — but it needs no batteries.

While these blocks are simple to make, they require some time to paint. You may want to make only three or four — just enough to spell out a special word or a name.

Colors Shown:

1. OFF WHITE
2. ANTIQUE WHITE
3. PURE RED
4. GREEN OLIVE
5. GOLDEN HARVEST
6. ULTRAMARINE BLUE
7. EQUAL PARTS OFF WHITE AND ULTRAMARINE BLUE
8. EQUAL PARTS OFF WHITE AND PARADISE BLUE
9. BARN RED
10. EQUAL PARTS PURE RED AND SUNKISS YELLOW
11. MUSTARD SEED
12. SOFT BLACK
13. STONEWARE BLUE
14. SOLDIER BLUE
15. EQUAL PARTS OFF WHITE AND GREEN OLIVE
16. EQUAL PARTS GREEN OLIVE AND BARN RED

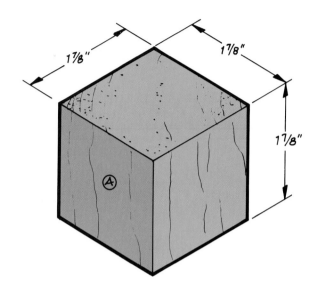

Special Tools

Backsaw, to cut the blocks
Miter box, to guide the backsaw

Shopping List

8/4 hardwood stock (approximately 1 board foot for an entire set of 13 blocks)

Paint

CUTTING LIST

A. Blocks
(as required) 1⅞" x 1⅞" x 1⅞"

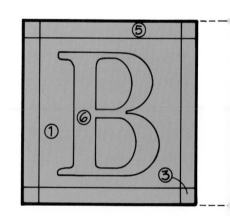

FULL SIZE PATTERNS

1. Choose and prepare the materials. Buy a good, stable hardwood for this project — one that won't change shape after you cut it. Poplar, maple, and birch are all good choices. You can find these at most lumberyards that carry hardwoods.

Note: Avoid using construction lumber. Construction-grade pine and fir is not thoroughly dried. The blocks may split, crack, or become distorted as they lose more moisture. This may happen weeks or months after you cut them — and all the time you spent painting them will be lost.

Ask the yardman for 8/4 (eight quarters) stock. This is wood that has been rough-sawed 2" (eight quarters on an inch) thick. Have him plane it to 1⅞" thick and joint (smooth and straighten) one edge for you. If he also provides a cutting service, have him rip the wood into strips 1⅞" wide.

❖

2. Cut the wood into blocks. If you didn't have the wood ripped at the lumberyard, cut it into strips with a handsaw. Then cut the strips into blocks with the backsaw and miter box. Most miter boxes have a slot for 90° cuts. Use this to cut the blocks perfectly square. (See Figure 1.)

❖

3. Sand the blocks smooth. Staple a piece of 80-grit sandpaper to a wide, flat board. Rub the sawed faces of the block on the sandpaper to remove the saw marks. (See Figure 2.) Replace the 80-grit sandpaper with 100-grit, and finish-sand *all* the surfaces of the blocks. Holding a small piece of sandpaper in your hand, slightly round the edges and corners of the blocks. They shouldn't have any sharp points.

❖

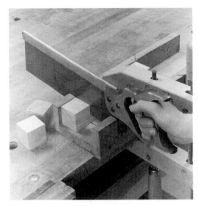

Figure 1. Use the 90° slot in the miter box to guide the backsaw when you cut the blocks. This will help you make perfectly square blocks.

Figure 2. Because the blocks are so small, it's easier to rub the blocks against the sandpaper than it is to rub the sandpaper against the blocks.

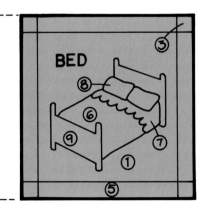
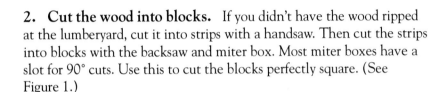
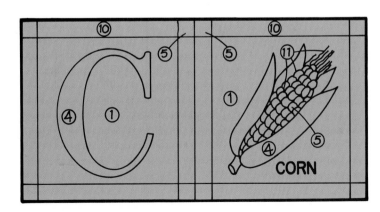

FULL SIZE PATTERNS

4. Paint the blocks. Transfer the patterns to the *sides* (face grain) of the blocks. You don't have to enlarge the patterns, since these are printed full size.

Leave the top and bottom (end grain) of each block blank. End grain is much harder to color than face grain because it soaks up the

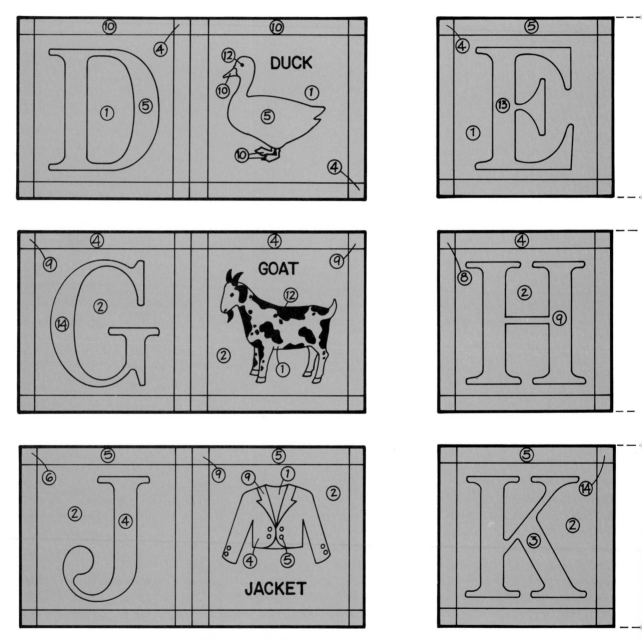

FULL SIZE PATTERNS

paint. To save time, apply a solid color to the top and bottom. Paint the letters and the pictures on the sides as suggested, or make up your own color scheme. If you wish, apply a protective coat of clear varnish or polyurethane to the painted blocks.

❖

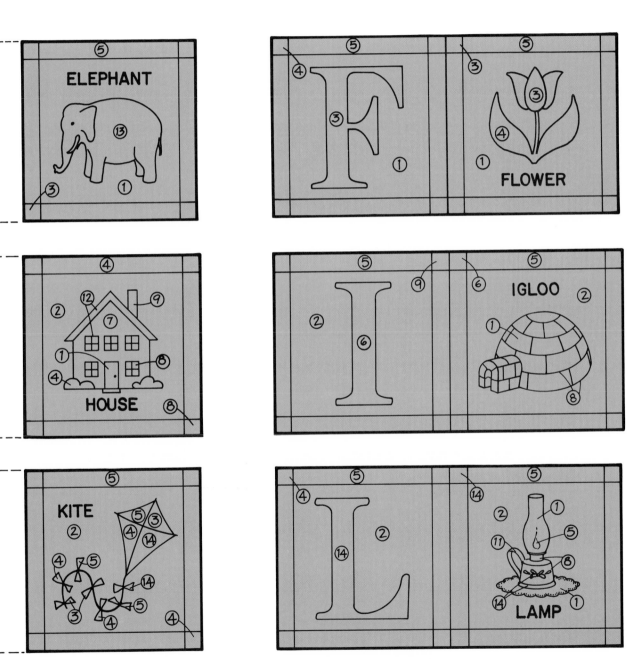

FULL SIZE PATTERNS

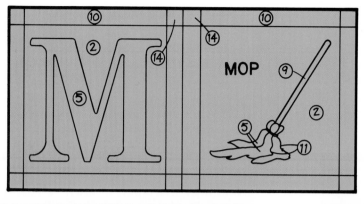

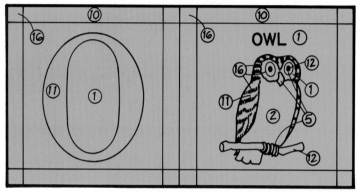

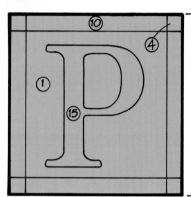

FULL SIZE

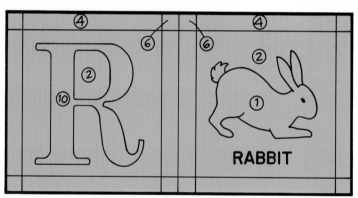

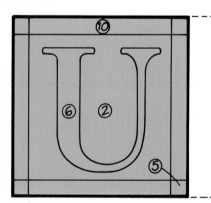

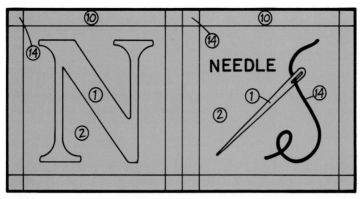

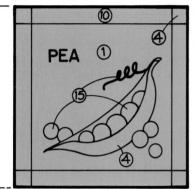

PATTERNS

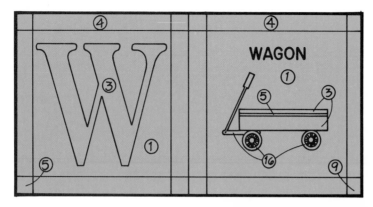

WAGON

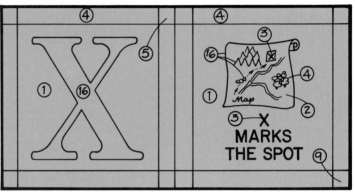

X
MARKS
THE SPOT

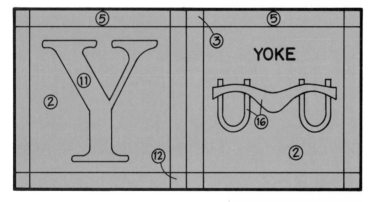

YOKE

**FULL SIZE
PATTERNS**

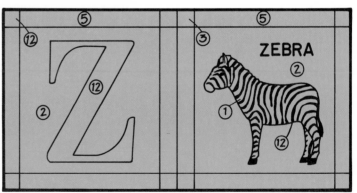

ZEBRA

COMB BOX

ver practical, country folk kept household items and tools near the place where they were used. If there wasn't a place to store them, they invented one. The comb box is just such an invention.

It's really not a box; rather, it's a small shelf or tray attached to a grooming mirror. This shelf holds combs, brushes, razors, and other toiletry articles right where you need them, whenever you need them. With your brushes and combs ready and waiting by the mirror, it's no trouble to give your hair a fresh part.

This particular comb box combines whimsy with practicality. With a little imagination, you can see the mirror as a window and the shelf as a flower box. So why not add a row of flowers to complete the image? The blooms add color, turning an otherwise utilitarian object into a piece of folk art.

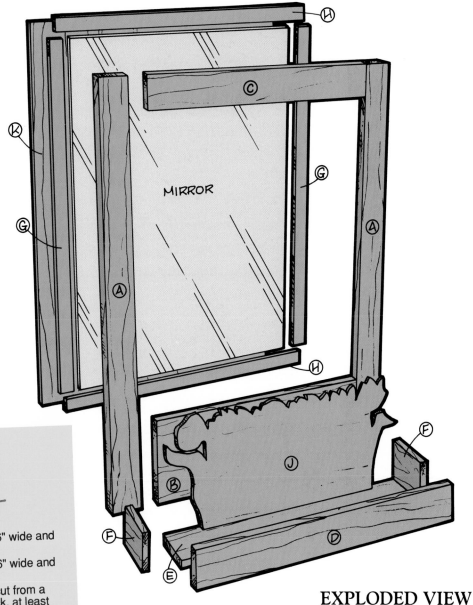

MIRROR

EXPLODED VIEW

Special Tools

None required

Shopping List

½"-thick stock (at least 6" wide and 48" long)

¼"-thick stock (at least 6" wide and 13½" long)

⅛"-thick stock (can be cut from a scrap of ¾"-thick stock, at least 2" wide and 18" long)

⅛"-thick hardboard (at least 13" wide and 16½" long)

⅛"-thick mirror (11⅜" x 14⅞")

1" wire brads (12–16)

½" wire brads (30–36)

¼" eyescrews (2)

Braided picture hanging wire (16"–18")

Picture hooks (2)

Carpenter's (yellow) glue

Paint

CUTTING LIST

A.	Frame stiles (2)	½" x 1½" x 20½"	F.	Sides (2)	½" x 2" x 3"
B.	Lower frame rail	½" x 4½" x 11"	G.	Side ledger strips (2)	⅛" x ¾" x 15"
C.	Upper frame rail	½" x 1½" x 11"	H.	Upper/lower ledger strips (2)	⅛" x ¾" x 13"
D.	Front	½" x 2" x 14"	J.	Flower cutout	¼" x 6" x 13½"
E.	Bottom	½" x 3" x 13"	K.	Mirror backing	⅛" x 13" x 16½"

Figure 1. When ripping thin pieces with a handsaw, you must be very careful not to let the saw wander. If it does, the piece may be too thin in some spots and too thick in others.

1. Choose the materials. If you plan to paint the comb box frame and shelf, you can make the parts out of almost any wood. If you want to stain them, white pine, maple, and birch all take a stain well. If you're just going to finish them, use a hardwood with an interesting grain pattern. Cherry and walnut will both look good. Avoid oak; the grain is too busy and will clash with the flower design.

Use hardboard for the mirror backing. (This is sometimes referred to as Masonite™.) If at the lumberyard you're asked whether you want tempered or untempered hardboard, choose tempered. It lasts longer.

For the flower cutout, use any *solid* wood. Avoid plywood; there are often voids and gaps in the edges. Even if you fill these with putty, a plywood cutout will not look as good as one made from solid wood.

Purchase the mirror at a glass shop. (Look in the Yellow Pages of your phone directory under "Glass.") Most of these shops will cut mirrors to size for you. They may also offer a choice of tinted mirrors, if you want something a little different.

❖

2. Cut the parts to size. Cut all the wooden and hardboard parts to the sizes in the Cutting List. Follow the Cutting Diagram when making the ½"-thick parts. This shows how to get all the parts from a single board with minimum waste.

To rip the ledger strips from a scrap of ¾"-thick stock, first scribe a line down the length of the stock, ⅛" from an edge. Clamp the stock to your workbench or a sawhorse so the edge overhangs. With a handsaw, cut to the *inside* of the line (opposite the edge). Cut slowly and carefully, following the line as precisely as possible. (See Figure 1.) Repeat until you have made all the ledger stock you need.

❖

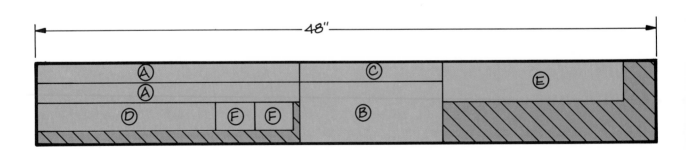

**CUTTING DIAGRAM
FOR ½" THICK PARTS**

3. Assemble the frame. Finish-sand the surfaces of the stiles and rails. Glue the ends of the rails to the edges of the stiles. Place the frame on a wide, flat surface, back side up.

Glue joints between the ends and edges are not very strong. You'll have to reinforce them. Otherwise, the frame may come apart. In this project, the glue joints are reinforced by the ledgers. These thin strips span the seams between the rails and stiles, holding them together.

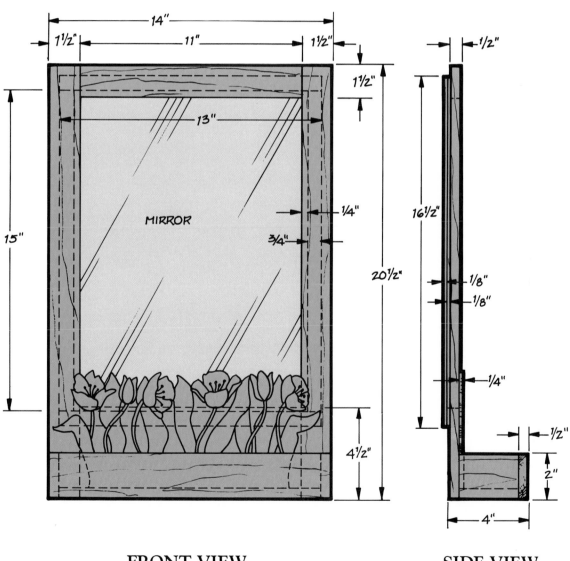

FRONT VIEW   **SIDE VIEW**

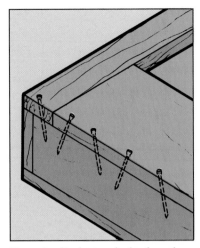

Figure 2. By driving the brads at alternating angles, you anchor the shelf to the frame. Even if the glue joint should break, the shelf will remain in place.

Glue the ledgers in place, ¼" from the *inside* edges of the frame, as shown in the Frame Joinery Detail. Tack the ledgers in place with ½"-long wire brads. Be sure to drive at least one brad on each side of each seam, wherever a ledger spans a joint.

4. Assemble the shelf. Finish-sand the surfaces of the front, bottom, and sides. Glue them together, reinforcing the joints with 1"-long wire brads. Let the glue dry completely.

Sand the joints on the frame and the shelf clean and flush. Then glue the shelf to the frame, flush with the bottom edge as shown in the Side View. Reinforce the glue joint with 1" brads. Drive the brads at slight angles, changing the angle for each brad. (See Figure 2.) This will help anchor the shelf to the frame.

With a wet rag, wipe away any glue that squeezes out of the joints. Let the remaining glue dry completely, then sand the joints clean and flush.

5. Cut the shape of the flowers. Enlarge the Flower Pattern and trace just the outside lines on the stock. Cut the shape with a saber saw or coping saw. Finish-sand the front surface and the sawed edges. If you wish, lightly carve the petals, leaves, and stems in the surface of the wood.

Note: The grain direction of the flower cutout should run side to side. When it's glued to the bottom rail, the grain of the two pieces must be parallel.

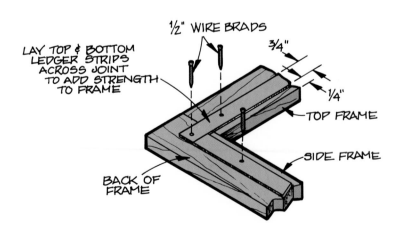

FRAME JOINERY DETAIL

6. Paint the comb box. Trace the interior lines of the Flower Pattern onto the cutout. Paint the flowers as suggested, or follow your own color scheme. Leave a small area unpainted on the *back* of the flower cutout, so you can glue it to the comb box. This area should be about 3" wide and 12" long, flush with the bottom edge and centered between the sides.

Also paint the comb box. Or, if you wish, apply a stain and a finish. Leave an area on the front of the bottom rail unfinished, to join to the unpainted area on the flower cutout.

❖

7. Attach the flowers and the mirror. Glue the flower cutout to the bottom rail. The bottom edge of the cutout should rest on the shelf bottom. Clamp the cutout in place while the glue dries.

Put the mirror between the ledger strips. Cover the ledgers and the mirror with the hardboard mirror backing. Tack — but *don't* glue — the backing to the ledgers with ½"-long wire brads. You want to be able to remove the backing, in case you break the mirror.

❖

8. Hang the comb box. Install two eyescrews on the back of the comb box, one in each stile, 4" to 5" from the top. Stretch a length of picture-hanging wire between the two screws.

Drive *two* picture hooks in the wall where you want to hang the comb box. The hooks should be level with each other and 9" to 10" apart. Hang the comb box from both hooks. This makes the mirror more stable, and you won't accidentally tilt it every time you reach for a comb or brush.

❖

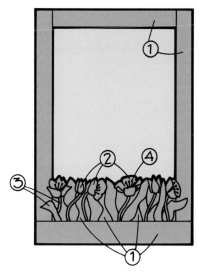

Colors Shown:
1. LIBERTY BLUE
2. JOSONJA RED
3. GREEN OLIVE
4. SOFT BLACK (STAMENS)

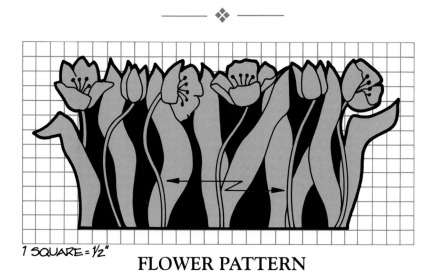

1 SQUARE = ½"

FLOWER PATTERN

CARRYALL

ne of the most useful accessories in the country home was the carryall, or caddy. Country folk used these handy trays to carry, organize, and store all sorts of small items — silverware, sewing notions, gardening tools, laundry supplies, and so on. Many homes had several carryalls, each with its specific purpose.

The carryall shown here is typical of many old-time carryalls. The construction is very simple. It's really just a box with a single divider. This divider is slightly higher than the sides of the box so that it can also serve as a handle.

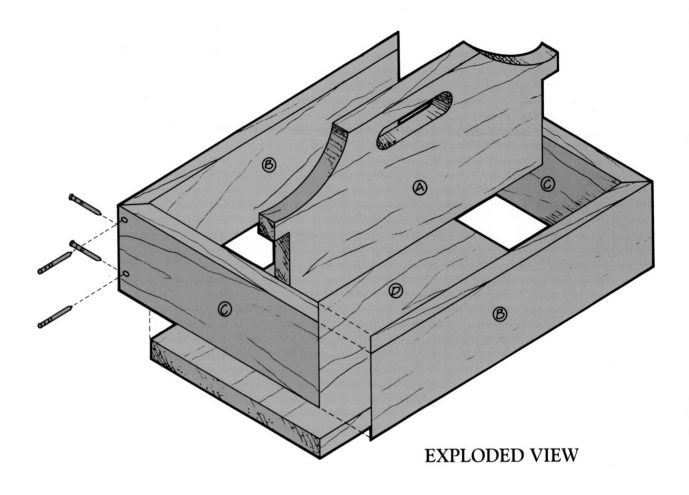

EXPLODED VIEW

Special Tools

A backsaw, to cut the miter joints at the corners

A miter box, to guide the backsaw

Note: The miter box and the backsaw aren't absolutely necessary. You can make a miter joint with a saber saw by tilting the foot. But you'll find that the miter box/backsaw does a much better job.

Shopping List

¾"-thick stock (a 1 x 8, at least 40" long)

¾"-thick plywood, approximately 10" x 14", grade A-C

4d finishing nails (16)

Carpenter's (yellow) glue

Medium and fine sandpaper

Paint

CUTTING LIST

A.	Handle	¾" x 6" x 14"
B.	Front/back (2)	¾" x 3½" x 14"
C.	Sides (2)	¾" x 3½" x 10"
D.	Bottom	¾" x 8½" x 12½"

1. Choose your materials. The front, back, sides, and handle of this project can be made from almost any domestic wood. Most were made from pine, walnut, cherry, or maple. We suggest that you use plywood for the *bottom* of the carryall because it is more stable than solid wood. That is, plywood doesn't expand with changes in temperature and humidity like solid wood does. If you use solid wood for the bottom, it will expand enough to pop the miter joints at the corners — and ruin your project.

— ❖ —

2. Cut the parts to size. Cut the parts to the dimensions in the Cutting List. The Cutting Diagram shows you how to make the front, back, sides, and handle from the 1 x 8 stock.

Miter the ends of the front, back, and sides at 45°, as shown in the Top View. (See Figure 1.) These parts should fit together like a picture frame.

— ❖ —

3. Cut the shape of the handle. Enlarge the Handle Pattern. Place a sheet of carbon paper, face down, between the pattern and the wood, then trace the shape onto the stock. Using a saber saw, cut out the scallops and the notches in the ends of this part. To make the opening for the handle, mount a 1" spade bit in your drill. Bore a 1"-diameter hole at each end of the handle opening outline. Then cut out the waste between the holes with a saber saw. (See Figure 2.) This woodworking technique is sometimes called a piercing cut.

— ❖ —

Figure 1. If you use a miter box and a backsaw to cut the miter joints, use very light pressure on the saw. If you use too much pressure, the saw will bind. Clamp the wood in the box to keep it from shifting.

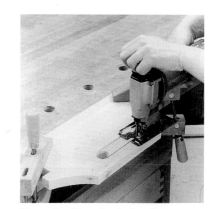

Figure 2. To make the handle opening, drill two holes approximately 3" apart, and cut out the wood between the holes.

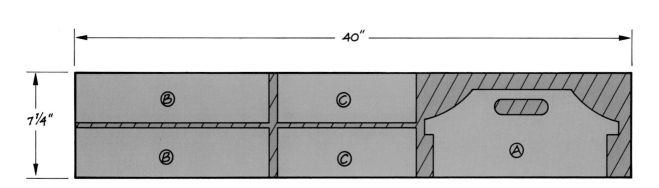

CUTTING DIAGRAM

40"

7¼"

Ⓑ Ⓒ

Ⓑ Ⓒ Ⓐ

4. Finish-sand the parts. Sand smooth the faces of all the parts. Also sand the inside of the handle opening to remove the saw marks. If you wish, round over the edges of the handle and the handle opening with sandpaper to make it more comfortable to use. Be careful not to round over edges or surfaces of any part that will later be joined to other parts.

❖

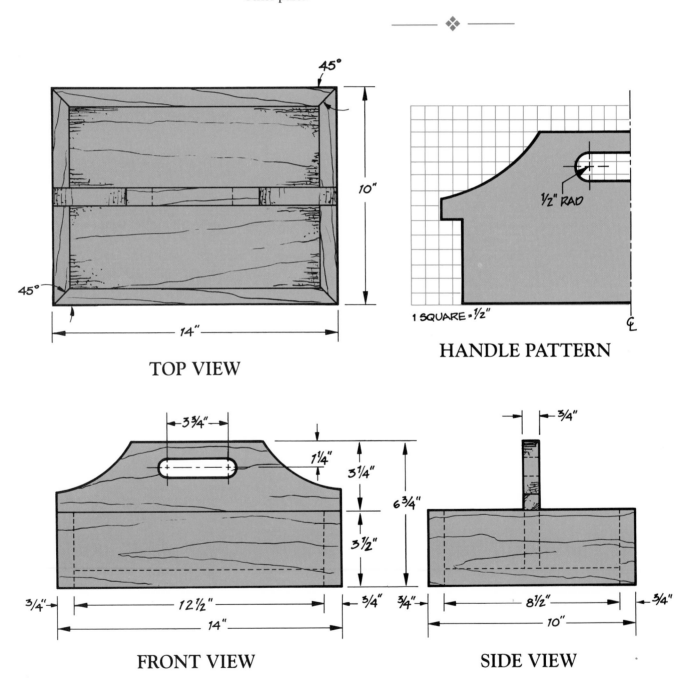

45°

45°

10"

14"

TOP VIEW

½" RAD

1 SQUARE = ½"

C̶L

HANDLE PATTERN

3¾"

1¼"

3¼"

6¾"

3½"

3/4"

12½"

14"

3/4"

FRONT VIEW

3/4"

3/4"

8½"

10"

3/4"

SIDE VIEW

5. Assemble the carryall. Glue the front, back, and sides together, then reinforce the miter joints with 4d finishing nails. Drive several nails into each corner, from *both* directions. The nails must cross at right angles, as shown in the Exploded View. (See Figure 3.) Glue the bottom to the box assembly, and secure it in place with finishing nails. Then attach the handle/divider to the box with glue and nails. With a wet rag, clean up any excess glue that may have squeezed out of the joints. Let the glue joints dry completely.

———— ❖ ————

6. Paint the completed carryall. Lightly sand the surfaces of the carryall to touch up any areas where parts don't quite fit, or to remove any glue you didn't wipe away. Then paint the completed carryall. You can use the pattern we show here, or choose another.

———— ❖ ————

Figure 3. To reinforce the miter joint drive finishing nails at right angles to each other. This will make it almost impossible to pull the corners apart.

1 SQUARE = ½"

PATTERN FOR PAINTING CARRYALL

Colors Shown:
① VILLAGE GREEN (BASE COLOR)
② PENNSYLVANIA CLAY
③ L'ORANGERIE
④ OFF WHITE

BIRD DECOYS ❖

Bird decoys served two different purposes, one aesthetic, the other practical. You can easily guess the aesthetic purpose — the decoys made wonderful decorations. They still do. But they also provided our early settlers with income and food. During the eighteenth and nineteenth centuries, feathers were high fashion. Inhabitants of rural and coastal areas used the decoys to trap birds — not just game birds, like ducks and pheasants, but many smaller birds as well. They plucked these and sold the feathers to buyers who would come out from the big cities from time to time. Then, true to their "waste not, want not" ethic, the trappers boiled the small carcasses, stripped them of meat, and baked it in a "peep" pie.

The decoys you see here are similar to those used to trap birds along the Atlantic coast. They represent several common shorebirds — a whimbrel, a killdeer, and a golden plover.

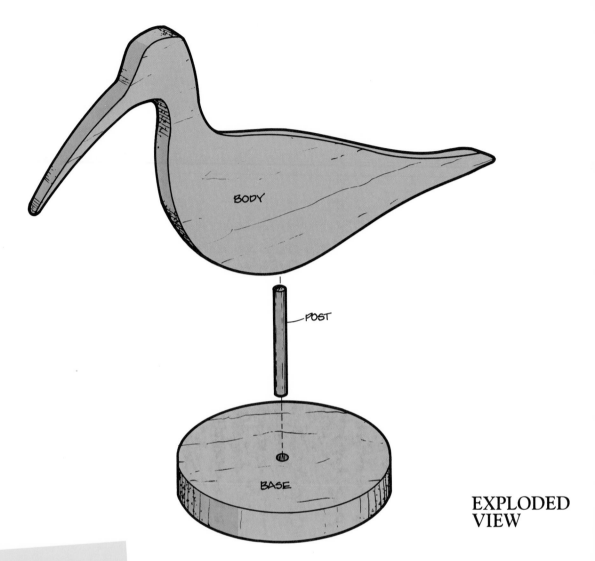

BODY

POST

BASE

EXPLODED VIEW

CUTTING LIST

A.	Whimbrel body	¾" x 5½" x 11"	F.	Plover base	4" diameter x ¾"
B.	Whimbrel post	¼" diameter x 3½"	G.	Killdeer body	¾" x 3½" x 7½"
C.	Whimbrel base	5" diameter x ¾"	H.	Killdeer post	¼" diameter x 2½"
D.	Plover body	¾" x 4½" x 9"	J.	Killdeer base	3" diameter x ¾"
E.	Plover post	¼" diameter x 3"			

1. Choose your materials. To shape the birds' bodies, you must do a little woodcarving. To make the carving easier, select a soft wood. The easiest wood to carve is basswood, which is available at many hobby stores and most lumberyards that carry hardwoods. If you can't get basswood, clear white pine is also a good choice.

Note: The amount of ¾"-thick wood specified in the Shopping List will make all three birds. If you wish to make only one or two of the birds, you don't need to purchase quite so much lumber.

❖

2. Cut the body and base parts to their rough sizes. Using a handsaw, cut the large ¾"-thick board into smaller pieces. These pieces should be the same size or a little larger than the sizes shown for the bodies and the bases in the Cutting List.

❖

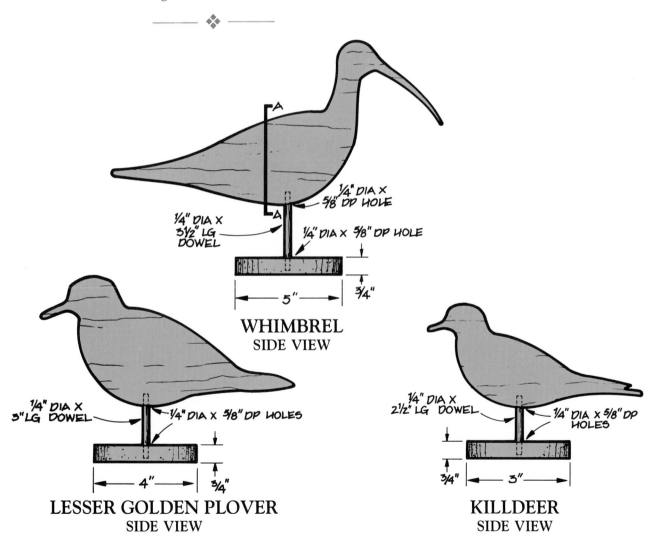

A

¼" DIA X 5/8" DP HOLE

¼" DIA X 3½" LG DOWEL

¼" DIA X 5/8" DP HOLE

5"

¾"

WHIMBREL
SIDE VIEW

¼" DIA X 3" LG DOWEL

¼" DIA X 5/8" DP HOLES

4"

¾"

LESSER GOLDEN PLOVER
SIDE VIEW

¼" DIA X 2½" LG DOWEL

¼" DIA X 5/8" DP HOLES

¾"

3"

KILLDEER
SIDE VIEW

LESSER GOLDEN PLOVER

1. WHITE WASH
2. WICKER
3. RAW SIENNA AND
   WHITE WASH
4. EQUAL PARTS SOFT
   BLACK, RAW SIENNA AND
   WHITE WASH
5. SOFT BLACK

KILLDEER

1. WHITE WASH
2. MUSTARD SEED
3. MUSTARD SEED &
   GOLDEN HARVEST
4. RAW SIENNA
5. RAW SIENNA DARKENED
   WITH RAW UMBER
6. SOFT BLACK

3. Cut the body shapes. Enlarge the patterns for the birds' bodies onto a piece of paper. Be sure to enlarge the entire pattern, including the interior lines and the location of the post holes. Trace the outside shape of the bodies onto the wood, then put the full-size paper patterns aside for the time being.

Cut the shapes of the bodies with a saber saw. Sand the sawed edges to remove the saw marks.

❖

4. Cut the shapes of the bases. With a compass, mark the circular shapes of the bases on the stock. Cut the bases with a saber saw, and sand the sawed edges.

❖

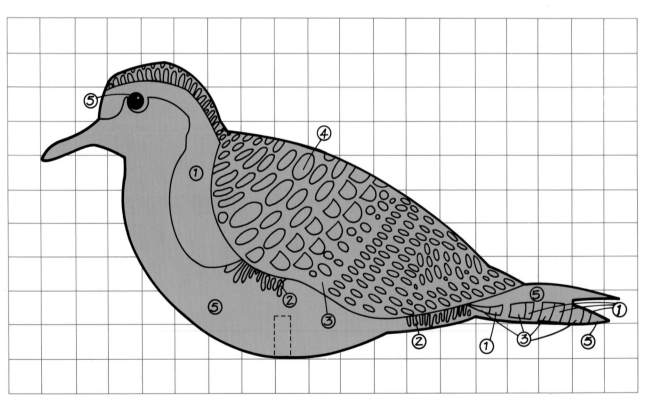

1 SQUARE = ½"

**LESSER GOLDEN PLOVER
PATTERN**

5. Drill the post holes. Lay the paper patterns on the birds' bodies and mark the locations of the post holes. Also, mark the locations of the post holes in the center of the bases.

Mount a ¼" drill bit in your drill to make the post holes. To keep from making these holes too deep, wrap a piece of masking tape around the bit, ⅝" from the end. When you bore the holes, stop the drill when the tape is even with the surface of the wood. (See Figure 1.)

——————— ❖ ———————

Figure 1. You'll get better results when drilling the post holes in a bird's body if you first clamp the body to your workbench. Wrap a piece of masking tape around the drill bit to gauge the depth of the hole.

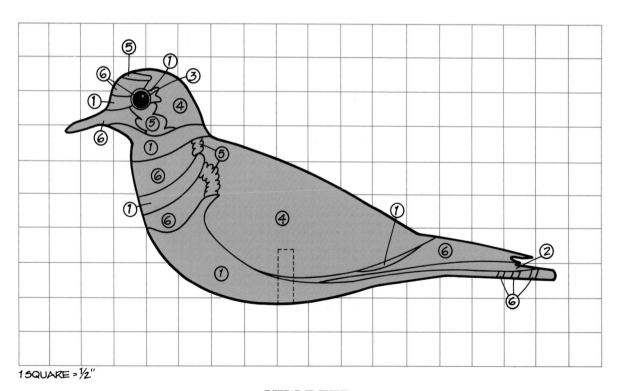

1 SQUARE = ½"

KILLDEER
PATTERN

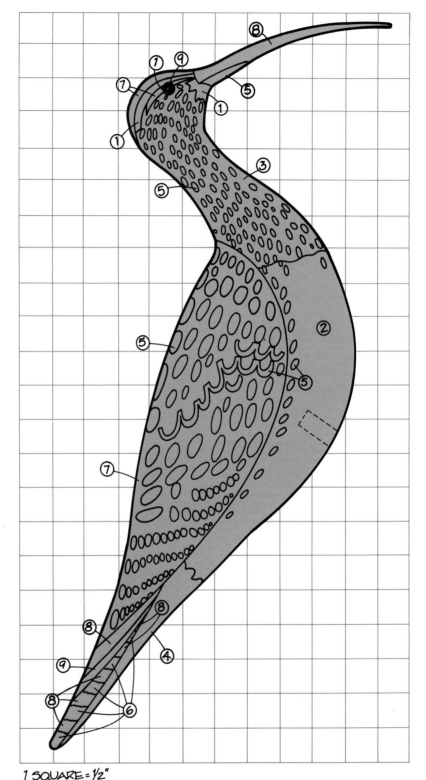

Colors Shown:

WHIMBREL

1. WHITE WASH
2. EQUAL PARTS ANTIQUE WHITE AND WHITE WASH
3. ANTIQUE WHITE
4. EQUAL PARTS ANTIQUE WHITE, WICKER AND WHITE WASH
5. EQUAL PARTS ANTIQUE WHITE AND WICKER, DARKENED WITH BURNT SIENNA
6. EQUAL PARTS RAW UMBER AND MUSTARD SEED, LIGHTENED WITH WHITE
7. EQUAL PARTS RAW UMBER, BURNT SIENNA AND WHITE WASH
8. EQUAL PARTS RAW UMBER AND SOFT BLACK LIGHTENED WITH WHITE
9. SOFT BLACK

1 SQUARE = 1/2"

WHIMBREL PATTERN

6. Carve the birds' bodies. Once the bodies have been sawed and drilled, they must be carved so that they are slightly oval-shaped, as shown in Section A. This doesn't require any special carving skills, but it does take time and patience.

Use a carving knife to shave the edges of the bodies. Remove just a little bit of wood at a time, until you get the shape you want. As you work, pay attention to the direction of the wood grain. If the knife wants to dig in, you're probably cutting into the grain, or "uphill," as some carvers call it. Turn the piece so that you always cut away from the grain, or "downhill." (See Figures 2 and 3.) When you have carved the bodies to their rough shape, sand the surface to remove the chisel marks.

❖

7. Cut the posts. Saw the ¼"-diameter dowel stock to the lengths needed for the posts. Lightly sand the ends of the posts to remove any wood splinters.

❖

8. Paint the birds. Tape the paper patterns to the birds' bodies with a piece of carbon paper in between the pattern and the wood. With a ballpoint pen, trace the interior lines of the pattern. The carbon paper will transfer these lines to the wood.

Paint the bodies to the colors shown. Study the color photo to choose the proper shades for each part of each body. You will find it useful to consult a good bird-watcher's guide — there are many such guides at your local library. Paint the posts and the bases a dark charcoal — almost black.

❖

9. Assemble the decoys. When the paints dry, put a little dab of glue on each end of each post. Insert the posts in the bases, then mount the bodies on the posts.

❖

Figure 2. If you carve into the grain, your knife will want to dig in.

Figure 3. Carving will be easier and the results better if you always cut away from the grain.

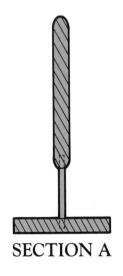

SECTION A

DOOR HARP

ountry folk took pleasure in the simple things. Even the opening or closing of a door could be a cause for celebration. In many country homes, a door harp would musically announce the comings and goings of friends and relations.

Door harps descended from the simple stringed zithers of German and Scandinavian immigrants to America. They have three or four wire strings, tuned to a chord and stretched across a sounding board. Each string has its own striker — a wooden bead hung so that it almost touches the wire. You "play" the harp by hanging the instrument on a door. When the door is moved, the beads swing away from the strings, then drop back and strike the chord. This creates a soft, tinkling sound every time the door is opened or closed.

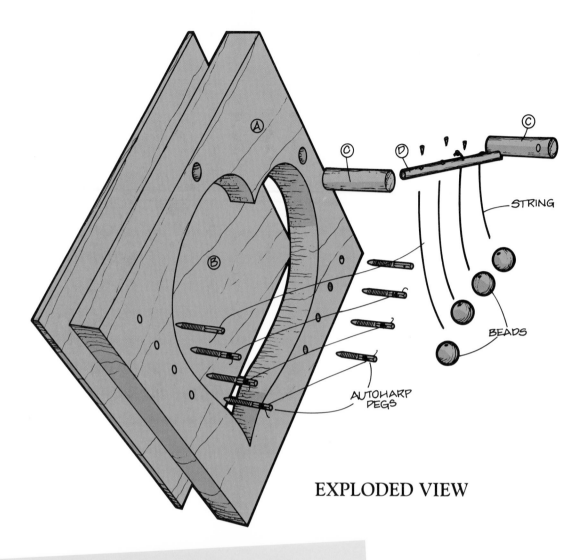

EXPLODED VIEW

STRING

BEADS

AUTOHARP
PEGS

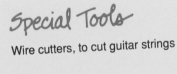

Special Tools

Wire cutters, to cut guitar strings

Shopping List

¾"-thick stock (1 x 10, 10" long)
⅛"-thick stock, 10" x 10"
¾"-diameter wooden beads (4)
½"-diameter wooden dowel, 4" long
¼"-diameter wooden dowel, 6" long
Autoharp pegs (8)
#12 steel guitar or banjo strings (2)
Nylon kite string (20")
Toothpicks (4)
#8 x 1" roundhead wood screw
Carpenter's (yellow) glue
Medium and fine sandpaper
Paint

CUTTING LIST

A.	Harp body	¾" x 9" x 9"
B.	Sounding board	⅛" x 9" x 9"
C.	Posts (2)	½" diameter x 1½"
D.	Stretcher	¼" diameter x 5"

1. Select and purchase the materials. Door harps can be made from almost any domestic hardwood. The one shown is built of poplar, but you can also use cherry, walnut, maple, or oak. Avoid softwoods, such as pine and fir. Softwoods will not grip the autoharp pegs tightly, and the strings will not stay tuned.

Purchase the ¾"-thick stock you need from any lumberyard that carries hardwoods. Obtain the ⅛"-thick stock from a mail-order woodworking supply company. The steel strings and the autoharp pegs can be purchased at most music stores. If you can't find the pegs locally, they can be bought through the mail from several musical instrument and woodworking supply houses. See Appendix B for a list of mail-order companies.

2. Cut the wooden parts to size. Cut the body, sounding board, posts, and stretcher to the sizes given in the Cutting List.

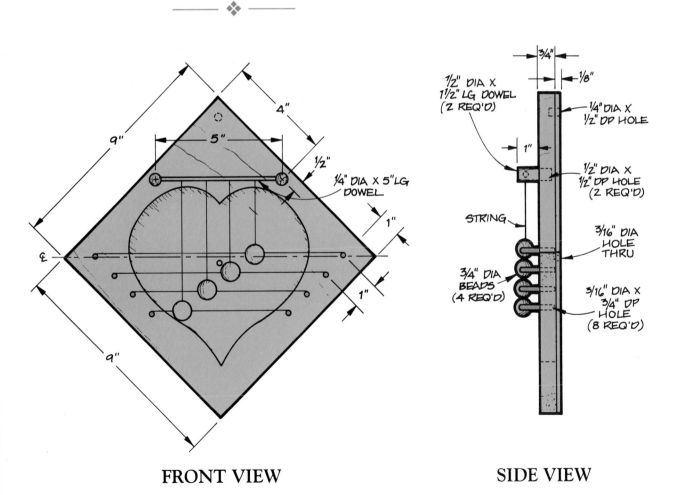

FRONT VIEW   **SIDE VIEW**

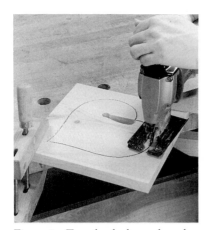

Figure 1. To make the heart-shaped sound hole, first drill a 1"-diameter hole in the waste, then insert the saw blade through this hole and cut the shape. This woodworking technique is called a piercing cut.

3. Cut the shape of the body. Enlarge the body pattern onto a piece of paper. Be sure to enlarge the entire pattern, including the interior lines and the locations of the post holes. Trace just the heart shape of the sound hole onto the wood, and put the full-size paper pattern aside for now.

Drill a 1"-diameter hole inside the outline of the heart shape. Insert the blade of a saber saw into this hole and cut out the shape. (See Figure 1.) Sand the sawed edges to remove the saw marks.

❖

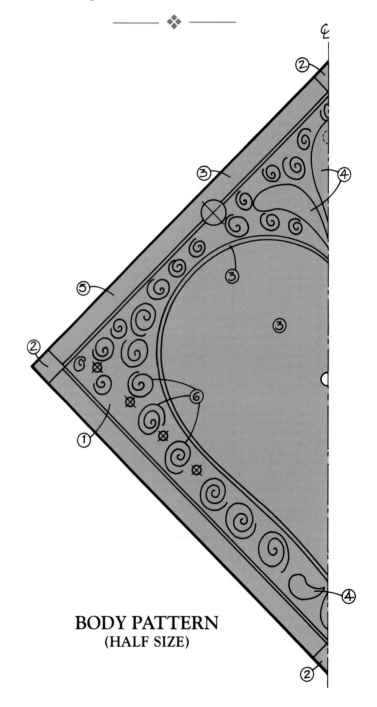

BODY PATTERN
(HALF SIZE)

Colors Shown:

① TELEMARK GREEN (BACKGROUND AND SIDES)

② COTTAGE ROSE (ALSO SIDES OF HEART AND BEADS)

③ APRICOT STONE

④ EQUAL PARTS COTTAGE ROSE AND APRICOT STONE

⑤ VILLAGE GREEN (ALSO POSTS & STRETCHER)

⑥ VILLAGE GREEN THINNED WITH WATER

4. Attach the sounding board to the body. Finish-sand the faces of the sounding board and the body. Spread glue on the back of the body, and clamp it to the sounding board. Wipe away any excess glue with a wet rag.

After the glue dries, remove the clamps. Sand the edges of the assembly so that the edges of the sounding board are flush with the edges of the body.

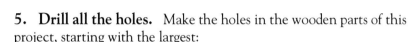

5. Drill all the holes. Make the holes in the wooden parts of this project, starting with the largest:

- Two ½"-diameter x ½"-deep holes in the front of the harp to hold the posts
- ¼"-diameter x ½"-deep hole in the back of the harp to hang it on a door
- Two ¼"-diameter x ⅜"-deep holes in the ends of the posts to hold the stretcher
- Eight ³⁄16"-diameter x ¾"-deep holes in the front of the harp to hold the autoharp pegs
- ³⁄16"-diameter hole through the sounding board to secure the harp to a door
- Four ⅛"-diameter x ⅜"-deep holes, one in each wooden bead to insert the string
- Four ⅛"-diameter holes through the stretcher to hang the wooden bead

To the right are some tips to help you drill these holes.

6. Paint the harp. Tape the paper pattern to the front of the harp with a piece of carbon paper face down between the pattern and the wood. With a ballpoint pen, trace the pattern lines. The carbon paper will transfer these lines to the wood. Paint the harp as shown, using artist's acrylics or oils. Also, paint the posts, the beads, and the stretcher.

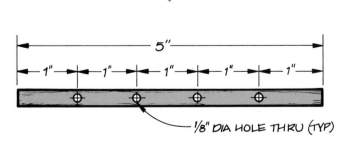

½" DIA HOLE THRU (TYP)

STRETCHER LAYOUT

TIPS
FOR DRILLING HOLES

❖ *Most of the holes for this project are "stopped" — that is, they don't go clear through the wood. Wrap a piece of tape around your drill bit to help judge the depth of these holes.*

❖ *When making holes in round dowel stock, hold the stock in a homemade V-jig to keep the dowel from rolling around the workbench. (See Figure 2.)*

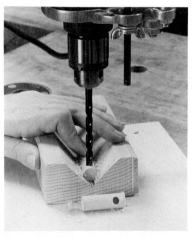

Figure 2. To hold round stock steady while you work on it, place it in a V-jig. You can make your own jig by sawing a V-shaped groove in a scrap of 2 x 4.

❖ *Most autoharp pegs require ³⁄16"-diameter holes. A few require slightly larger holes. Check the diameter of the hole recommended by the peg manufacturer before you drill. If none is recommended, measure the diameter of the pegs and drill holes ¹⁄32" smaller.*

7. Assemble the posts and stretcher. Apply a little glue to both ends of the stretcher, to one end of the posts, and to the holes that hold both the stretcher and the posts. Before the glue sets, assemble the posts and stretcher to the harp. Check that the ⅛"-diameter holes in the stretcher are oriented up and down, parallel with the harp body. Wipe off any excess glue with a wet rag — a little water won't hurt the paint.

8. Attach and tune the strings. Using a pair of pliers, drive the autoharp pegs into their holes as if they were screws. The pegs have extremely fine threads, and they will turn down like screws — they just take a lot longer. Stop turning when the tiny holes in the pegs are ⅜" above the surface of the harp.

Cut the steel guitar strings in two, so you have four lengths. Tie a length very loosely between two pegs. Double-loop each end of the length of string through the hole in its peg, as shown in the Peg Detail. This will keep the strings tight when you tune them. Repeat until you have strung four sets of pegs.

Carefully tighten each string. Turn the peg at the left end of the string counterclockwise one revolution, then turn the peg at the right end clockwise one revolution. Repeat until the string is taut enough to sound a note when you pluck it. Do this for all four strings.

Tune the strings so they sound a chord when plucked in unison. The top string should sound the base note of the chord, the next string the third, and the next the fifth. The last or bottom string should sound the octave. If you don't have a musical ear, get somebody who plays the piano or a stringed instrument to help you do this.

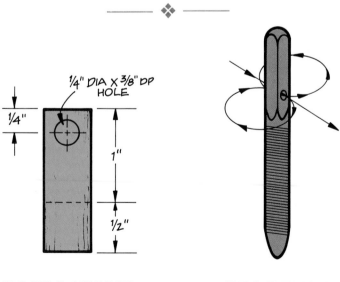

POST LAYOUT   **PEG DETAIL**

9. Hang the wooden beads. Cut four lengths of kite string. Insert one end of one string into the ⅛"-diameter hole in a wooden bead. Dip one end of a toothpick in glue, and drive it into the hole so that it wedges the string in place. Then break the toothpick off, leaving the end in the hole.

Temporarily clamp or brace the door harp so the body is vertical and the strings are horizontal — the same position in which you will hang the harp. Insert the other end of the string in one of the ⅛"-diameter holes in the stretcher. Pull the string through the hole so that the wooden bead hangs directly beside one of the tuned guitar strings. With the other end of the toothpick, wedge the kite string in the stretcher. Break off the toothpick and cut off the dangling end of the kite string.

Repeat this for all four wooden balls. Each ball must be hung beside a different guitar string, so that all four strings will be struck when the door harp is moved.

— ❖ —

10. Hang the door harp. Touch up the paint on the harp, if necessary. Drive a small nail in the door where you want to hang the harp, and place the harp so that the ¼" hole in the back fits over the nail. Drive a roundhead wood screw through the ³⁄₁₆" hole in the sounding board and into the door. This will hold the harp tight against the door as it's opened and closed.

— ❖ —

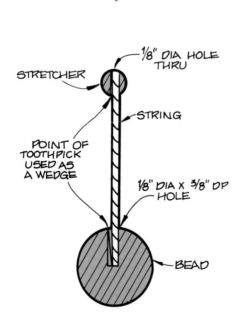

STRETCHER

⅛" DIA HOLE THRU

STRING

POINT OF TOOTHPICK USED AS A WEDGE

⅛" DIA X ⅜" DP HOLE

BEAD

BEAD/STRETCHER DETAIL

LADDER SHELVES

urprisingly, country craftsmen did not often build shelves. Our ancestors didn't need them as much as we do. The library of a typical eighteenth- or nineteenth-century country home consisted of a single book — the Bible. Knickknacks were rare. To be able to collect such things — and to have the room to display them — was a luxury that few could afford.

When they did build shelves, they made small, wall-hung racks like this one, designed to store particular items, such as plates and dishes. They were called by many different names, the first of which was "cup boards." Later, the term *cupboard* was borrowed to describe large, standing kitchen cabinets, and small, hanging shelving units became plate racks and pewter shelves. Sometimes, when the shelves were narrow and evenly spaced, as they are in this project, they were called ladder shelves.

The design for these ladder shelves was adapted from a piece made by an anonymous New England craftsman in the early eighteenth century. (It's now on display at the Winterthur Museum near Wilmington, Delaware.) The distinctive profile of the sides was characteristic of classic William and Mary furniture, the predominant style at that time.

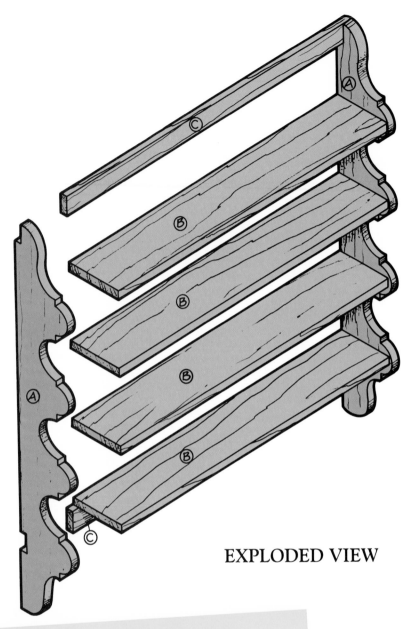

EXPLODED VIEW

Special Tools

None required

Shopping List

½"-thick stock (2 pieces, at least 6"
   wide and 108" long)
#8 x 1¼" flathead wood screws
   (24–30)
⁵⁄₁₆"-diameter dowel (about 12" long)
Molly anchors (2)
Carpenter's (yellow) glue
Paint, stain, or finish

CUTTING LIST

A. Sides (2)   ½" x 6" x 40"
B. Shelves (4)   ½" x 6" x 23"
C. Braces (2)   ½" x 2" x 24"

1. Choose the materials. If you plan to paint the ladder shelves, you can make the parts out of almost any wood. If you want to stain them, white pine, maple, and birch all take a stain well. If you're just going to finish them, use a hardwood with an interesting grain pattern. Cherry and walnut will both look good. Avoid using oak; country craftsmen didn't often build with oak.

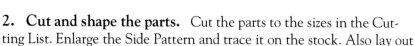

2. Cut and shape the parts. Cut the parts to the sizes in the Cutting List. Enlarge the Side Pattern and trace it on the stock. Also lay out the notches on the sides, as shown in the Side View. These notches must be precisely 2" wide and ½" deep. Cut the shapes of the parts, using a saber saw or a coping saw. Sand the sawed edges smooth.

   Tip: The braces must fit snugly in the notches. To get them to fit just right, cut the notches a little small, sawing just inside the lines. Then file the stock up to the lines. (See Figure 1.)

Figure 1. To fit a brace to a notch, saw the notch a little small. Enlarge the notch with a file, test fitting the brace from time to time. Stop when the brace fits just right.

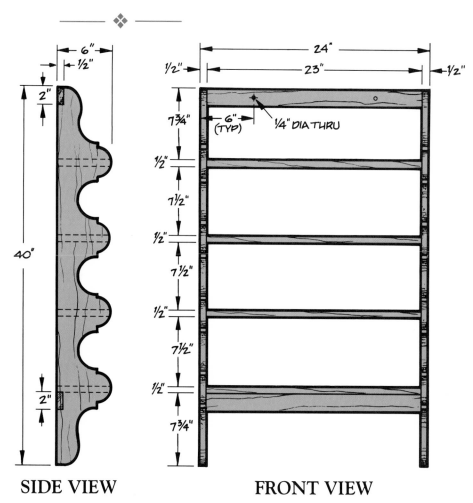

SIDE VIEW   **FRONT VIEW**

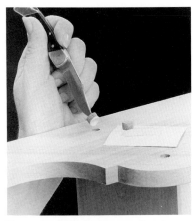

Figure 2. To hide the screw heads, glue dowel plugs in the counterbores. After the glue dries, sand or file the plugs flush with the wooden surface.

3. Drill the mounting holes. Measure and mark the mounting holes in the upper brace, as shown in the Front View. Drill ¼"-diameter holes through the brace at the marks.

4. Assemble the shelves. Finish-sand the faces of all the parts. Carefully mark the positions of the shelves on the surface of each side. Glue all four shelves to a single side, reinforcing the joints with screws. Then attach the other side. Finally, attach both braces. Glue and screw the lower brace to the lower shelf as well as to the sides.

Use the screw drill to counterbore and countersink the screw heads. The counterbores should be about ¼" deep, so the heads will rest below the surface. With a coping saw, cut the ⁵⁄₁₆"-diameter dowel into ³⁄₈"-long plugs. Dip these plugs in glue and press them into the counterbores, covering the screw heads. (See Figure 2.)

With a wet rag, wipe off any glue that squeezes out of the joints or from around the plugs. Let the remaining glue dry. File and sand the plugs even with the wood surface, as shown in the Screw Joinery Detail.

5. Paint or finish the ladder shelves. Lightly sand the assembled shelves to clean the surfaces, then paint or finish them. Traditionally, pieces like these were painted with milk paint. Several companies still make old-time milk paint, and it is available at most paint stores and arts and crafts supply centers. If you don't paint the ladder shelves, stain them or apply a clear finish.

6. Hang the ladder shelves. Position the shelves on the wall where you want them to hang. With a pencil, mark the locations of the mounting holes. Put the shelves aside, and drill ¼"-diameter holes through the wall where you've marked it. Insert a molly anchor in each hole, then tighten the bolt on the end of the molly. You'll be able to feel the anchor expand inside the wall.

Back the bolts out of the mollies and insert them through the mounting holes in the shelves. Position the shelves on the wall, over the molly anchors. Drive the bolts back into the mollies, fastening the ladder shelves securely to the wall.

Note: Molly anchors will work for *most* (but not all) situations. If you position one of the mounting holes over a 2 x 4 stud in the wall, use a #8 x 2" roundhead wood screw in this hole. If the wall is built from some other material besides wood, plaster, or drywall, ask the clerk at your local hardware store to recommend suitable anchors.

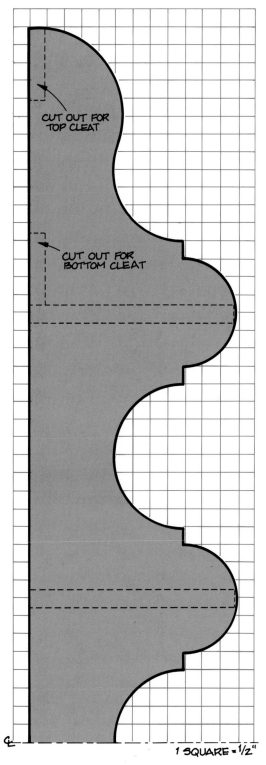

CUT OUT FOR
TOP CLEAT

CUT OUT FOR
BOTTOM CLEAT

1 SQUARE = 1/2"

SIDE PATTERN

COUNTERBORE

#8 X 1¼"
FHWS

PLUG

COUNTERSINK

PILOT
HOLE

SCREW JOINERY DETAIL

TRUMPETING ANGEL WIND VANE

ithout televised forecasts, country folk relied on the direction of the wind to predict the weather. A gentle breeze from the southwest usually meant a sunny day ahead; a strong wind from the northeast often brought rain. A quick change in the wind direction sometimes preceded a violent storm or blizzard.

Almost every barn and public building was fitted with a wind vane. These vanes came in many sizes and shapes — running horses, crowing roosters, spouting whales, shooting stars — the list is almost endless. The trumpeting angel was a popular design, particularly among the German immigrants of Pennsylvania. The angel you see here is a smaller version of an old wind vane now in the Mercer County Museum near Mercer, Pennsylvania.

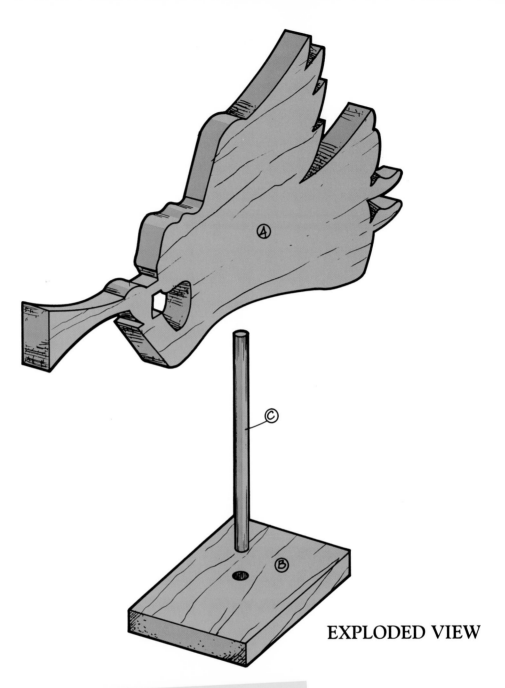

EXPLODED VIEW

Shopping List

¾"-thick stock (1 x 8, at least
    24" long)
¼"-diameter dowel, 8" long
Carpenter's (yellow) glue
Medium and fine sandpaper
Paint

CUTTING LIST

A. Angel   ¾" x 7¾" x 16"
B. Base   ¾" x 4" x 6"
C. Dowel   ¼" diameter x 7"

TRUMPETING ANGEL
WIND VANE

1. Choose the materials. Select a soft wood, such as white pine or basswood, to make the angel-shaped wind vane. These woods are easier to cut and shape than many other species.

——— ❖ ———

2. Cut the parts to size. Cut the angel, base, and dowel to the sizes specified in the Cutting List. Sand the ends of the dowel to remove any splinters.

——— ❖ ———

3. Cut the angel shape. Enlarge the pattern for the angel onto a piece of paper. Be sure to enlarge the entire pattern, including the interior lines and the location of the holes. Place a sheet of carbon paper over the stock and trace just the outside shape onto the stock. Put the full-size paper pattern aside for now.

Cut the shape of the body with a saber saw. Sand the sawed edges to remove the saw marks.

——— ❖ ———

Colors Shown:

1. METALLIC SILVER (UNDERCOAT)
2. ROSEBERRY
3. EQUAL PARTS PEACHES N' CREAM AND OFF WHITE
4. OFF WHITE (POST)
5. WILD HONEY
6. STONEWARE BLUE AND OFF WHITE

STONEWARE BLUE (BASE)

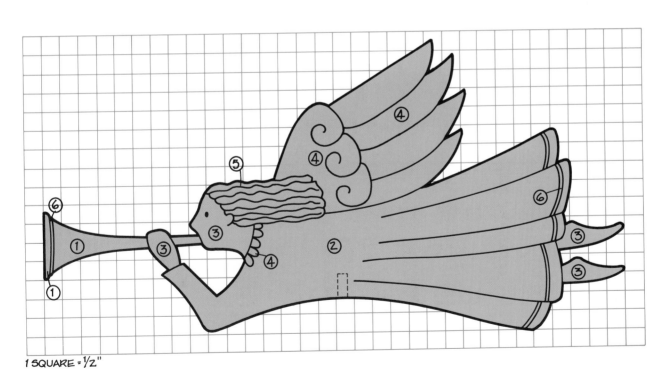

1 SQUARE = 1/2"

ANGEL PATTERN

4. Drill the mounting holes. Mount a ¼" drill bit in your drill to make the mounting holes. To keep from making these holes too deep, wrap a piece of masking tape around the bit ⅝" from the end. When you bore the holes, stop the drill when the tape is even with the surface of the wood. Drill two holes, one in the angel and the other in the base, as shown in the Front View.

5. Paint the parts. Tape the paper pattern to the angel, placing a piece of carbon paper between the pattern and the wood. With a ball-point pen, trace the interior lines of the pattern. The carbon paper will transfer these lines to the wood.

Paint the angel with a thin coat of silver acrylic paint and let dry. Apply colored paint to a small area, then, before the color dries completely, rub the area with a clean cloth to remove some of the paint.

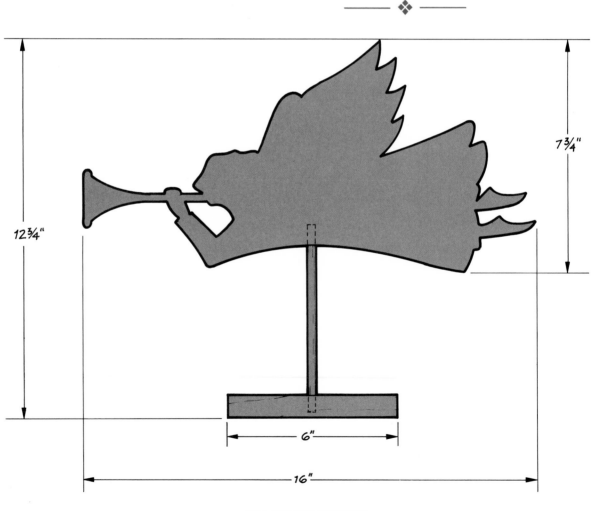

FRONT VIEW

TRUMPETING ANGEL
WIND VANE

Continue in this manner until the angel is colored as shown. The silver paint will shine through the colors, making them shimmer.

Paint the post white and the base a sky blue.

6. Assemble the wind vane. When the paint dries, put a little dab of glue on the ends of the post. Insert the post in the base, then mount the angel on it.

Note: This is a decorative, *non-working* wind vane — that is, it doesn't turn with the wind. For the wind vane to work, it must be mounted on a metal pivot. If you want a functional wind vane, see the Watermelon Man Whirligig for instructions on how to make a pivot.

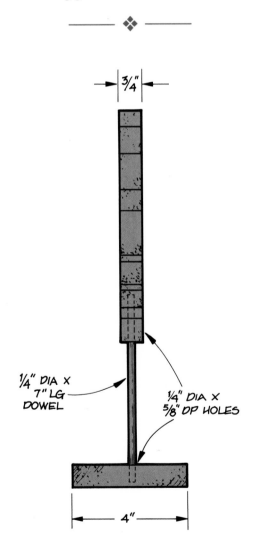

END VIEW

PUTZ VILLAGE

mong the many folk traditions the German immigrants brought with them to this country was the *putz*. (It rhymes with "roots.") This was a miniature village of houses, shops, and barns. Traditionally, the settlers displayed it under their Christmas trees. However, many putz villages sat out all year round on mantels and windowsills.

The buildings could be of any size; there was no set scale. Often a *putz* mixed many different scales. There were no set designs, either. Sometimes a German craftsman made a village to resemble his own adopted American home. More frequently it was a fairy-tale village, a fanciful remembrance of the Old World towns and hamlets he left behind.

This *putz* is smaller and plainer than most. But it's also easier to make. The houses are wooden blocks, cut to various angles and glued together. Windows, doors, and other architectural details are painted on.

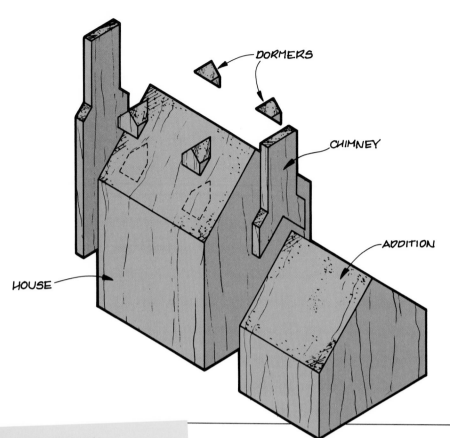

DORMERS

CHIMNEY

ADDITION

HOUSE

EXPLODED VIEW

Special Tools

Combination square, to guide the handsaw
Backsaw, to cut angles of the roofs
Miter box, to guide the backsaw

Shopping List

3"-thick stock (about 3 board feet of carving stock to make all 8 buildings)
Carpenter's (yellow) glue
Paint

CUTTING LIST

#1 House

| A. | House | 1½" x 3½" x 4" |
| B. | Chimneys (2) | ½" x ½" x ¾" |

#2 House

A.	House	1½" x 3" x 6"
B.	Chimneys (4)	¼" x ¼" x 1"
C.	Dormers (4)	½" x ¾" x ¾"

#3 House

A.	House	3" x 3" x 4⅜"
B.	Addition	2¼" x 3" x 3"
C.	Tall chimney	¼" x 1¼" x 5"
D.	Short chimney	¼" x 1¼" x 2½"
E.	Dormers (4)	½" x ½" x ½"

#4 House

| A. | House | 2" x 2⅝" x 3" |
| B. | Chimneys (2) | ¼" x ⅜" x 3" |

#5 House

A.	House	2½" x 3½" x 3¾"
B.	Addition	1½" x 2" x 3½"
C.	Chimney	¼" x 1" x 4½"

#1 Barn

A.	Barn	3" x 3½" x 4¼"
B.	Addition	¾" x 1¾" x 2¾"
C.	Cupolas (2)	¾" x ¾" x ¾"

#2 Barn

A.	Barn	3" x 3½" x 4"
B.	Addition	1" x 1⅞" x 3"
C.	Cupola	1" x 1" x 1"

Shed

| A. | Shed | 1½" x 2" x 2⅜" |
| B. | Chimney | ¼" x ⅜" x 2¾" |

1. Choose the materials. Buy a good, stable wood for this project — one that won't change shape after it's cut. The wood should also be fairly soft, making it easy to cut and shape the parts of the houses, barns, and shed. The best choice is basswood, followed by butternut and lauan mahogany. These woods are available in large, thick blocks from most hardwood lumberyards, some arts and crafts stores, and mail-order outlets for woodcarving supplies.

Note: Avoid using construction lumber. Construction-grade pine and fir is not thoroughly dried. The buildings may split, crack, or become distorted as they lose more moisture. This may happen weeks or months after you cut them — and all the time you spent making them will be lost.

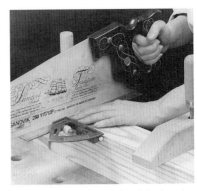

Figure 1. Rest the blade of the handsaw against the combination square as you cut. This will keep the blade perpendicular to the surface of the wood.

2. Cut the parts to size. Decide which of the buildings you want to make. Cut the parts to the sizes in the Cutting List. Use a handsaw to make the larger parts, such as the houses, barns, and additions. To cut the blocks perfectly square, use a combination square to guide the saw. Start your cut and saw about ⅛" deep. Place the square on the block and hold it in place with one hand. With the saw in the other hand, rest the blade against the upright arm of the square. Start sawing, keeping the saw pressed against the square. (See Figure 1.)

Cut the smaller parts — chimneys, dormers, cupolas, trees, and shrubs — with a backsaw and a miter box. These parts are too small to cut with a handsaw; it's too difficult to grasp them while you saw them. A miter box, however, holds small stock for you while you slice it with the backsaw. (See Figure 2.)

Figure 2. Most miter boxes have 90° slots to make square cuts as well as angled cuts. This is useful when cutting small stock.

3. Cut the shapes of the parts. Shape all the large parts by cutting miters and bevels with a backsaw. These angles create the slopes of the roofs. On a few buildings, you can use the miter box to guide the saw. On most, however, you must cut freehand. Carefully mark the shape of the house or barn on all sides. Clamp the stock to your workbench and saw very slowly. Follow the lines very carefully, taking care not to let the saw wander. (See Figure 3.) After finishing the cut, sand the sawed edges.

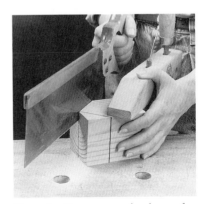

Figure 3. You must cut the slopes of the roof freehand, using a backsaw. This is not as difficult as it sounds. The trick is to mark the cut so you have lines to follow. Cut very slowly and don't let the saw wander off the lines.

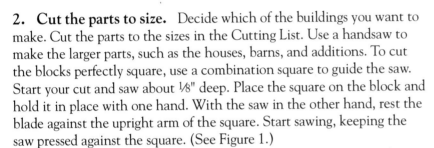

Figure 4. The dormers and the cupolas are too small to cut the angles accurately. Instead, *sand* the angles by rubbing them back and forth on a sheet of sandpaper.

Colors Shown:

ALL WINDOWS — SOLDIER BLUE
CHIMNEY TOPS — RAW UMBER

#1 HOUSE
SIDES AND CHIMNEYS — BRICK
ROOF — RAW UMBER
DOOR — WILD HONEY

#2 HOUSE
ROOF — RAW SIENNA
CHIMNEYS — BRICK
(SIDE A)
SIDES — MUSHROOM
DOOR — EQUAL PARTS
    ANTIQUE WHITE AND
    MUSTARD SEED
(SIDE B)
SIDES — WILD HONEY
DOOR — EQUAL PARTS
    MUSHROOM AND PINE
    NEEDLE GREEN

#3 HOUSE
SIDES — STONEWARE BLUE
DOORS — INDIAN SKY
ROOF — EQUAL PARTS
    SOFT BLACK AND OFF WHITE
CHIMNEYS AND STOOPS —
    WICKER

#4 HOUSE
SIDES — 1 PART GREEN OLIVE
           4 PARTS MUSHROOM
DOORS — GREEN OLIVE
ROOF — PINE NEEDLE GREEN
CHIMNEYS — 1 PART
    MUSHROOM AND 3 PARTS
    WHITEWASH

Cut the shapes of the chimneys with a coping saw. Once again, saw slowly and follow the lines carefully. Sand or file the sawed edges.

Sand — don't cut — the angles on the dormers and the cupolas. Staple a sheet of 80-grit sandpaper to a wide, flat board. Mark the shape of the part as if you were going to cut it. Instead, rub the part back and forth on the paper, grinding the angle you want. Stop when you grind the wood down to the pencil lines. (See Figure 4.)

❖

4. Assemble the buildings. Sand any surfaces that still need it. Rub the parts against a piece of sandpaper, in the same manner that you shaped the dormers and cupolas. Take care not to round the hard edges and sharp corners until after the buildings are assembled.

Glue the additions to the buildings first, clamping the parts together. Then glue the small parts — dormers, chimneys, and cupolas. Tape these parts in place until the glue dries. Sand all glue joints clean, and round the edges and corners.

❖

5. Paint the buildings. Lightly sand all the surfaces clean. Pencil the doors and windows on the building, as shown in the drawings. Paint the buildings as suggested, or make up your own color scheme.

❖

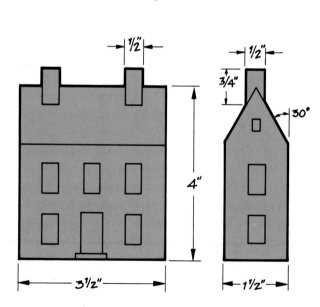

FRONT AND BACK VIEWS   **END VIEW**

#1 HOUSE

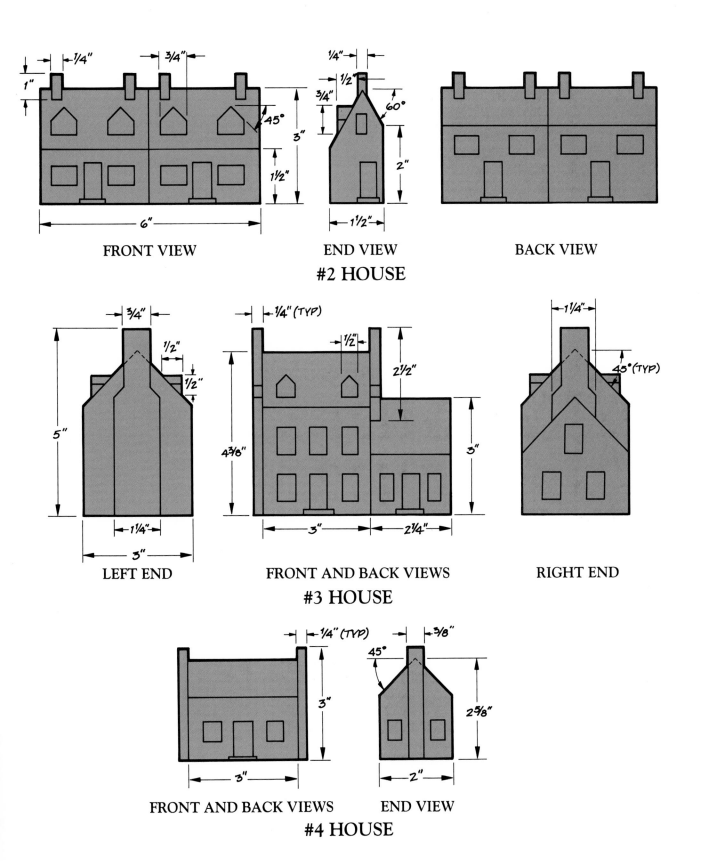

FRONT VIEW   END VIEW   BACK VIEW

#2 HOUSE

LEFT END   FRONT AND BACK VIEWS   RIGHT END

#3 HOUSE

FRONT AND BACK VIEWS   END VIEW

#4 HOUSE

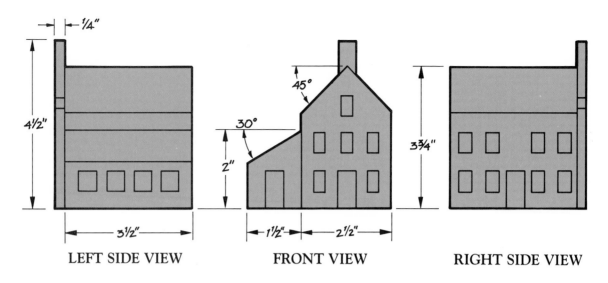

LEFT SIDE VIEW   FRONT VIEW   RIGHT SIDE VIEW

#5 HOUSE

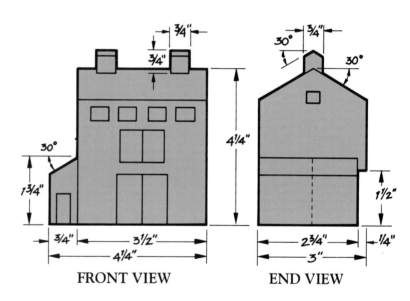

FRONT VIEW   END VIEW

Colors Shown:

#5 HOUSE
SIDES — WICKER
DOORS — OFF WHITE
ROOF — RAW UMBER
CHIMNEY — BRICK

#1 BARN
SIDES — EQUAL PARTS
  VICTORIAN MAUVE AND
  MUSHROOM
DOORS — EQUAL PARTS
  BRICK AND MUSHROOM
ROOF — RAW UMBER

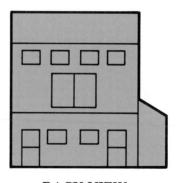

BACK VIEW

#1 BARN

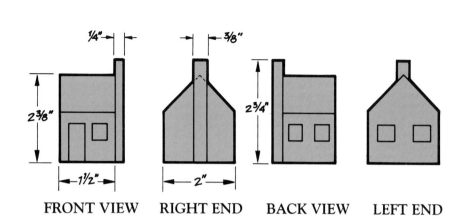

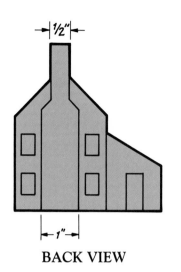

BACK VIEW

#5 HOUSE

FRONT VIEW   RIGHT END   BACK VIEW   LEFT END

SHED

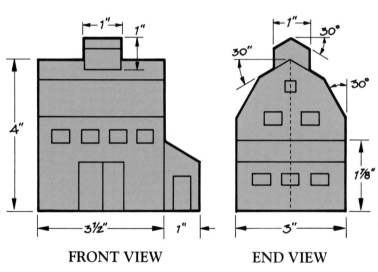

FRONT VIEW   END VIEW

(Paint opposite
end the same
except without
extension.)

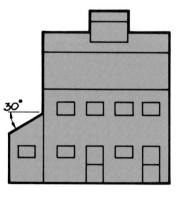

BACK VIEW

#2 BARN

Colors Shown:

SHED
SIDES — RAW SIENNA
DOORS — MUSTARD SEED
ROOF — EQUAL PARTS
  VICTORIAN MAUVE AND
  MUSHROOM
CHIMNEY — EQUAL PARTS
  ANTIQUE WHITE AND
  INDIAN SKY

#2 BARN
SIDES — BARN RED
DOORS — FINGERBERRY
ROOF — EQUAL PARTS
  APRICOT STONE AND
  MUSHROOM

SALT BOX

alt wasn't always stored in a shaker. Before the invention of iodized salt early in this century, untreated salt crystals clumped together. These clumps would have blocked the holes of a modern salt shaker, making dispensing the salt difficult, if not impossible.

Instead, a typical nineteenth-century cook kept her salt in a box with a wide opening at the top. Whenever she needed to add a little salt to a stew, she reached in for a pinch or two. For convenience, this box normally hung by the stove. A lid kept soot and grease from settling in the salt.

Salt boxes were made simply, so they could be replaced easily. Because they wore out quickly, owing to the constant use and the chemical action of the salt, the maker usually didn't even bother to attach the lid with hinges. Instead, he used strips of leather, bent wire, or metal scraps. The lid on the box you see here swings on cotter pins.

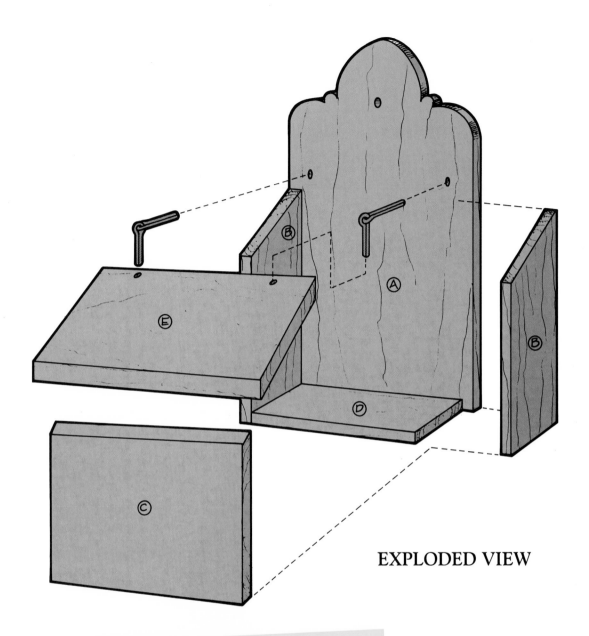

EXPLODED VIEW

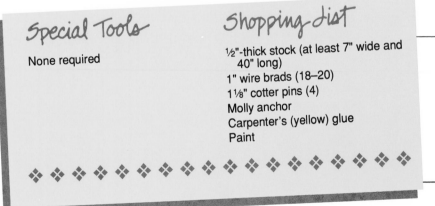

Shopping List

½"-thick stock (at least 7" wide and
   40" long)
1" wire brads (18–20)
1⅛" cotter pins (4)
Molly anchor
Carpenter's (yellow) glue
Paint

CUTTING LIST

A.	Back	½" x 7" x 12"
B.	Sides (2)	½" x 4" x 7"
C.	Front	½" x 7" x 5"
D.	Bottom	½" x 4" x 6"
E.	Lid	½" x 6" x 8½"

1. Choose the materials. Almost any wood can be used to make the salt box. Old-time craftsmen often made them from white cedar (sometimes called juniper wood). This is one of the few domestic woods that resists the decaying effects of salt. White cedar has become scarce, but you can still find it at some hardwood lumberyards. Cotter pins are available from any hardware or automotive parts store.

2. Cut the parts to size. Cut the wooden parts — back, front, sides, bottom, and lid — to the sizes shown in the Cutting List. Miter-cut the top end of each side at 60°, as shown in the Side View. Also bevel-cut the edges of the lid and the top edge of the front at 30°. (See Figure 1.)

Figure 1. To make bevel cuts, tilt the base (or "shoe") of your saber saw to the desired angle. Cut slowly, and clamp a straightedge to the wood to help guide the saw.

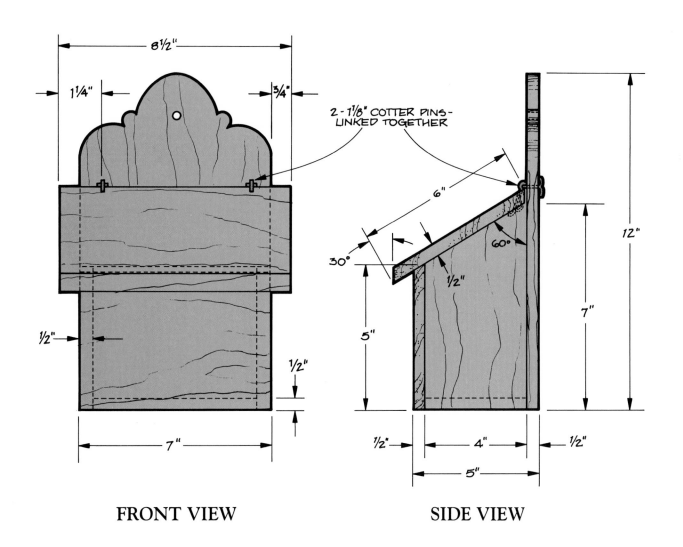

FRONT VIEW

SIDE VIEW

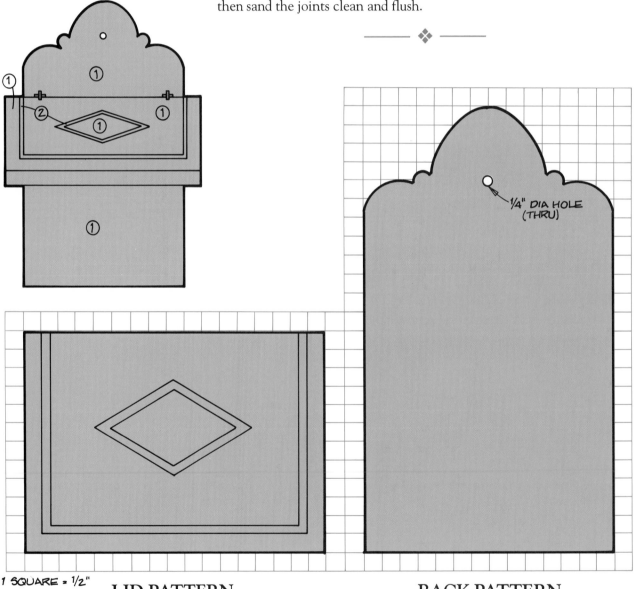

Colors Shown:

① BASE COLOR — TELEMARK GREEN

SPONGE PAINTING —
1ST LAYER — VILLAGE GREEN
2ND LAYER — GREEN OLIVE
3RD LAYER — DEEP FOREST GREEN

② VILLAGE GREEN

3. Cut and drill the back. Enlarge the Back Pattern, and trace it onto the stock. Be sure to mark the position of the mounting hole, too. Cut the shape of the back with a saber saw, then sand the sawed edges. Drill a ¼"-diameter mounting hole through the stock.

❖

4. Assemble the salt box. Finish-sand the faces of the wooden parts. Glue the back, front, sides, and bottom together, then reinforce the joints with 1"-long wire brads. Using a wet rag, wipe off any glue that squeezes out of the joints. Let the remaining glue dry completely, then sand the joints clean and flush.

❖

¼" DIA HOLE (THRU)

1 SQUARE = ½"   **LID PATTERN**   **BACK PATTERN**

5. Hinge the lid to the box. Drill two ⅛"-diameter holes in the upper edge of the lid. Each hole should be 1¼" in from the upper corners, as shown in the Front View. Angle the holes, entering the wood on the underside of the lid, ⅛"–¼" from the beveled edge. Exit at the edge, right in the point of the bevel. (See Figure 2.)

Place the lid on the salt box. Center it to overhang each side by ¾". Mark the locations of the holes on the back, remove the lid, and drill ⅛"-diameter holes straight through the back.

Connect two 1⅛"-long cotter pins together, joining the two looped ends as you would join paper clips or the links of a chain. (See Figure 3.) Repeat, making two sets of linked cotter pins.

Insert the straight end of a cotter pin in a hole in the lid, and bend it over on the underside. Repeat, fastening a cotter pin in the other hole. Then insert the two unattached cotter pins in the holes in the back. Bend them over on the back side. Test the action of the lid: It should raise and lower easily.

6. Paint the salt box. Straighten the cotter pins and remove the lid from the box. Also remove the cotter pins from the lid. Lightly sand the salt box and the lid, cleaning all the wood surfaces. Paint the salt box and the lid, using the suggested pattern and color scheme, or one of your own design. After the paint dries, reassemble the salt box and the lid with the cotter pins.

7. Hang the salt box. Position the salt box on the wall where you want it to hang. With a pencil, mark the location of the mounting hole. Put the box aside, and drill a ¼"-diameter hole through the wall where you've marked it. Insert a molly anchor in the hole, and tighten the bolt on the end of the molly. You'll be able to feel the anchor expand inside the wall.

Back the bolt out of the molly and insert it through the salt box mounting hole. Position the box on the wall, over the molly anchor. Drive the bolt back into the molly, fastening the salt box securely to the wall.

Note: A molly anchor will work for *most* (but not all) situations. If you position the mounting hole over a 2 x 4 stud in the wall, use a #8 x 2" roundhead wood screw to mount the salt box. If the wall is built from some other material besides wood, plaster, or drywall, ask the clerk at your local hardware store to recommend a suitable anchor.

Figure 2. It may take some practice before you can drill the cotter pin holes so they exit right where you want them. Drill several holes in scrap stock before you try it in good wood.

Figure 3. Pass one cotter pin through the looped end of the other, linking them as shown.

1⅛"
COTTER
PIN

HINGE DETAIL

ANIMAL TRIVETS AND CUTTING BOARDS

ife on a pioneer farm was hard, the hours were long, and any relief from the tedium was welcomed. So, fashioning even the most ordinary utensil was an opportunity for creativity. Many simple tools, such as these animal-shaped cutting boards, were decorated to provide a bit of color or whimsy as one went about his or her chores.

The utility of the item remained paramount, however. Decoration could not interfere with work. A realistic rendering of the sheep or a chicken would have produced boards that were too long and narrow to be useful. These fat caricatures aren't just an expression of country humor; they also show respect for the work that has to be done.

Special Tools

Woodburning tool, to decorate trivets (optional)

Shopping List

¾"-thick stock (1 x 10, at least 40" long)

Medium and fine sandpaper

CUTTING LIST

A.	Sheep	¾" x 8⅝" x 9"
B.	Cow	¾" x 8½" x 11"
C.	Pig	¾" x 7¼" x 10⅛"
D.	Chicken	¾" x 8½" x 9¾"

1. Choose your materials carefully. Because these boards will be used as cutting and chopping surfaces, they should be made from hardwood. And because they will be washed, they must withstand an occasional dunking. Finally, because you want to burn or paint a pattern on the boards, the wood should be light-colored.

There are two types of wood that fulfill all the above criteria — maple and birch. They are both very hard. The pores of the wood grains are "closed," so water can't soak into the stock. And the colors of these woods vary from light tan to creamy white. They are both common hardwoods, and are available at most lumber stores.

Note: The amount of ¾"-thick wood specified in the Shopping List will make all four cutting boards. If you wish to make only one or two, you don't need to purchase as much lumber.

2. Cut the boards to their rough sizes. Using a handsaw, cut the large ¾"-thick board into smaller pieces, the same size or a little larger than the sizes shown in the Cutting List.

3. Cut the shapes. Enlarge the patterns for each cutting board onto a piece of paper. Be sure to enlarge the entire pattern, including the interior lines. Trace just the outside shape onto the wood, and put the full-size paper patterns aside for now.

Cut the shapes of the bodies with a saber saw. Using a file, remove the saw marks from the sawed edges. (It's difficult to sand smooth the edges of very hard woods. A file makes this chore much easier.)

4. Burn or paint the animal shapes. Tape the paper patterns to the cutting boards with a piece of carbon paper in between each pattern and the wood. With a ballpoint pen, trace the interior lines of the pattern. The carbon paper will transfer these lines to the wood.

If you have a woodburning tool, trace the interior lines with a pointed tip. Switch to a broad, flat tip and shade in the areas shown in the patterns. (See Figures 1 and 2.) If you don't have a woodburning tool, you can use artist's acrylics or oils, instead. With a fine brush, trace the interior lines in a deep brown color. Let the lines dry, then fill in the shaded areas.

Figure 1. Most woodburning tools come with several interchangeable tips. Use a pointed tip to make sharp lines.

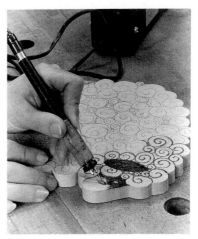

Figure 2. Use the long, flat edge of a broad tip for shading. Shading cools the tip quickly, so work slowly. Don't try to draw the tip across the wood too quickly.

1 SQUARE = ½"

PATTERN

5. Apply a finish. Because cutting boards are used to prepare foods, they require special, nontoxic finishes. There are two choices. The most common is mineral oil. The oil soaks into the wood and protects it from the inside out. Apply several coats, letting the boards dry for a few hours between each application.

Or: Use "salad bowl" finish. This is sold through several mail-order woodworking supply houses. (Refer to the Appendix for addresses.) Unlike the mineral oil, salad bowl finish builds up a protective coat on the outside of the wood. It's a particularly good finish to use if you have painted your cutting boards. The coating will protect both the wood and the paint.

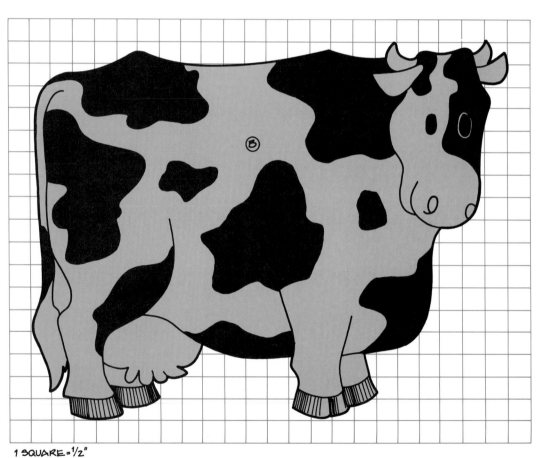

1 SQUARE = ½"

PATTERN

1 SQUARE = ½"

PATTERNS

WOODEN DOLL

Ever since there were children, adults have fashioned dolls for them. They made dolls from whatever materials were available — clay, rags, seed pods, cornhusks, and dried apples were some of the things they used. One of the most abundant resources on an American pioneer farm were trees. Consequently, many country dolls were created from wood.

These were usually simple toys, like the doll shown here. The features were more often painted than carved. The arms and legs were sometimes jointed at the shoulders and hips, but rarely at the elbows and knees. The clothes were made from scraps of homespun fabric, and were sometimes glued or tacked directly to the doll.

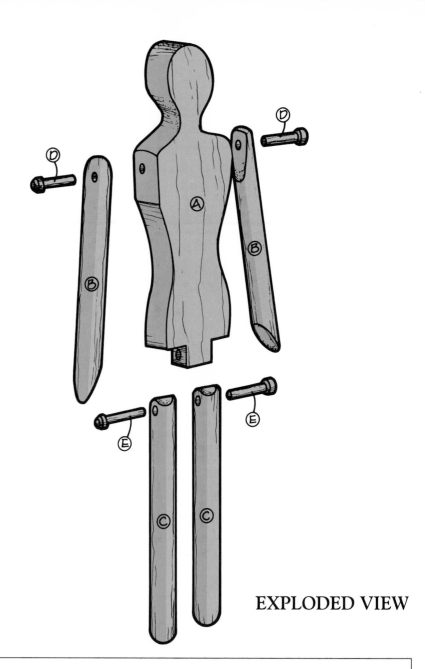

EXPLODED VIEW

Special Tools

Sewing machine, for making clothes (optional)

Shopping List

¾"-thick stock (1 x 3, 8" long)
½"-diameter dowel, 12" long
⅝"-diameter dowel, 12" long
7⁄32"-diameter wooden pegs
¼ yard colored fabric for dress
¼ yard white fabric for apron and petticoat
Lace or ribbon for trim
Carpenter's (yellow) glue
Medium and fine sandpaper
Paint
Thread

CUTTING LIST

Wooden Parts

A.	Body	¾" x 2" x 7¼"
B.	Arms (2)	½" diameter x 5⅛"
C.	Legs (2)	⅝" diameter x 5¾"
D.	Arm pegs (2)	7⁄32" diameter x 13⁄16"
E.	Leg pegs (2)	7⁄32" diameter x 11⁄16"

Fabric Pieces

F.	Petticoat	6⅝" x 14"
G.	Dress	10" x 12"
H.	Dress sleeves (2)	5¼" x 6"
J.	Apron	7½" x 8⅛"
K.	Apron sash	2" x 22"
L.	Apron bib	2⅜" x 4"

1. Choose the materials. You can make a wooden doll from almost any wood. However, it's best to choose light-colored stock, such as poplar or pine, since you'll be painting the doll. You can purchase both the ¾"-thick stock and the dowels at most lumberyards. Pegs can be bought at most hobby and craft stores. If you can't find them locally, they may have to be ordered from a mail-order woodworking supply house. (See the Appendix for a list of addresses.)

2. Cut the wooden parts to size. Cut the wooden parts to the sizes shown in the Cutting List. When you cut the pegs, measure the length of the shank *only*. *Do not* include the head. The size of the peg head varies slightly with each manufacturer, so this is not included in the Shopping List or Cutting List dimensions.

3. Cut the shape of the body. Make a photocopy of the full-size Body Pattern, and place it over the stock. Insert a sheet of carbon paper, face down, between the pattern and the wood. Trace just the outside shape onto the wood, and put the photocopied pattern aside for now.

Cut the body shape with a saber saw. Sand the sawed edges to remove the saw marks, and round over the edges with sandpaper.

4. Shape the ends of the arms and legs. Miter the upper ends of the arms, as shown in the Front View, so that they will angle away from the body slightly. To do this, first draw two intersecting lines on a piece of scrap wood. The angle between the lines must be 20°. Clamp an arm to the scrap of wood, parallel with one line. Cut it with a coping saw, keeping the saw parallel with the other line. (See Figure 1.) Miter the lower ends of the arms at 45°, using the same method. Sand the lower ends of the arms and both ends of the legs to round them, as shown in the drawings.

5. Drill the peg holes. Lay the paper pattern on the body and mark the locations of the peg holes. Mount a ⁷⁄₃₂"-diameter drill bit in your drill to make the holes. To keep from making the arm peg holes too deep, wrap a piece of masking tape around the bit, ½" from the end. When you bore these holes, stop the drill when the tape is even with the surface of the wood.

Switch to a ¼"-diameter bit and drill ¼" holes through the upper ends of the legs and arms where you want to peg them to the body.

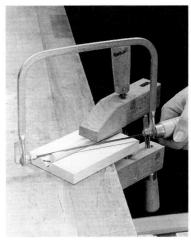

Figure 1. A V-block makes it easy to clamp round stock to a flat board. Lines on the board help you line up the arm and the saw.

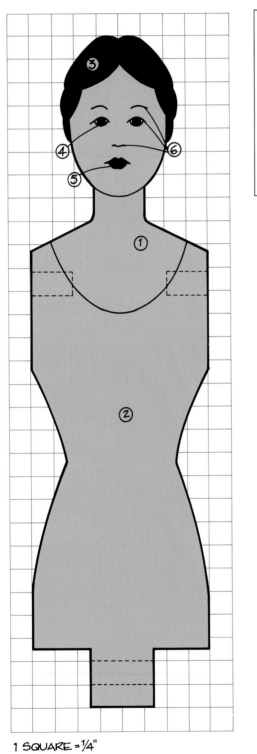

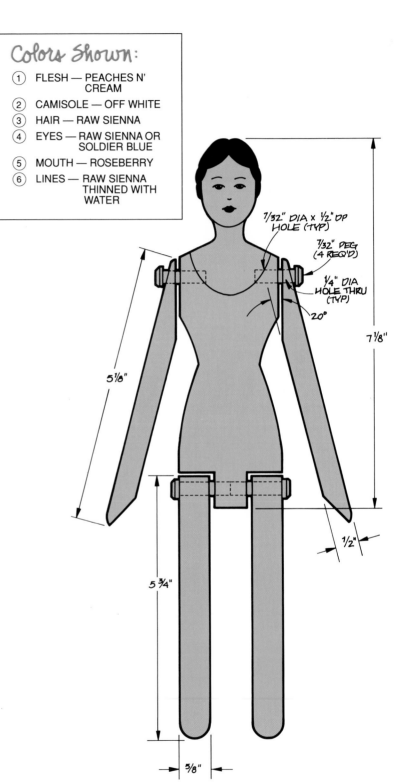

Colors Shown:

① FLESH — PEACHES N' CREAM

② CAMISOLE — OFF WHITE

③ HAIR — RAW SIENNA

④ EYES — RAW SIENNA OR SOLDIER BLUE

⑤ MOUTH — ROSEBERRY

⑥ LINES — RAW SIENNA THINNED WITH WATER

1 SQUARE = ¼"

BODY PATTERN
(FULL SIZE)

FRONT VIEW

7/32" DIA x ½" DP HOLE (TYP)

7/32" PEG (4 REQ'D)

¼" DIA HOLE THRU (TYP)

20°

7⅛"

5⅛"

5 ¾"

½"

5/8"

6. Assemble the doll. Finish-sand the arms, legs, and body. Dry-assemble the parts of the doll (without using any glue) to check that the arms and legs swing freely. If they don't, you may have to cut the shanks of the pegs slightly longer.

If they swing properly, take the doll apart again. Put a dab of glue into each peg hole in the body. Insert the pegs through the holes in the arms and legs, then put another dab on the end of each peg. Reassemble the doll, pressing the pegs into the holes in the body. Wipe away any excess glue so the arms and legs aren't accidentally glued to the pegs.

——— ❖ ———

7. Paint the doll. Tape the paper pattern to the body with a piece of carbon paper in between the pattern and the wood. With a ballpoint pen, trace the lines of the face. The carbon paper will transfer these lines to the wood.

Paint the wooden doll a flesh color all over. When this dries, paint the face and hair onto the doll. (The facial lines will show through the flesh-colored paint.) Also, paint shoes on the ends of the legs.

——— ❖ ———

8. Cut the fabric pieces. Enlarge patterns for the clothing and trace them on a piece of paper. Fold the fabric and lay the paper patterns on it, lining up the indicated edges with the fold. Mark all the dots, then cut out the fabric parts.

——— ❖ ———

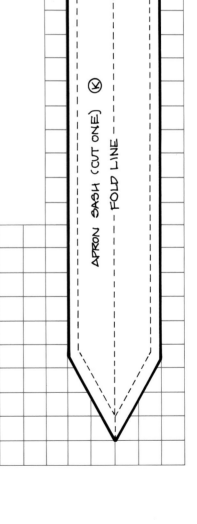

1 SQUARE = ½"

APRON PATTERN

9. Sew the petticoat. Stitch the side seam of the petticoat and sew lace to the bottom edge. Turn the top edge under where the pattern indicates it should be folded and sew on a casing. Stop about an inch before the starting point to leave an opening. Insert elastic or a drawstring in the casing to gather the waist.

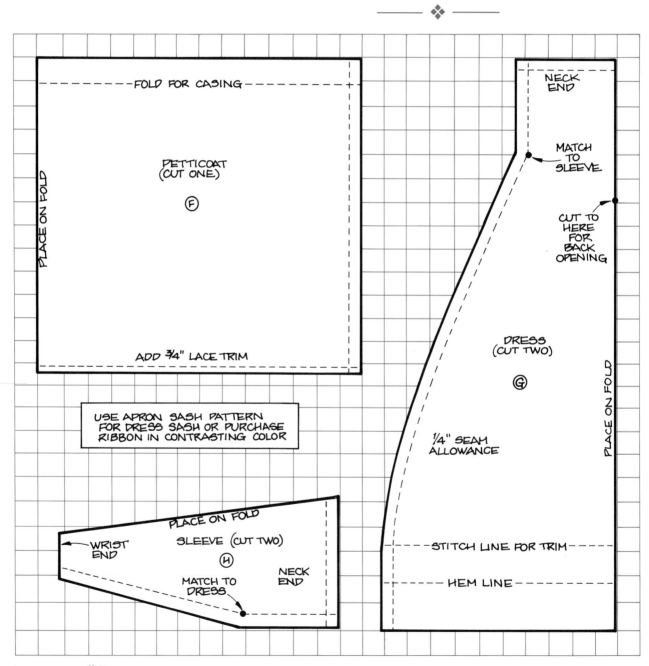

DRESS AND PETTICOAT PATTERN

10. Sew the dress. Pin one sleeve to the dress, right sides together, matching up the dots. Starting at the neck end, sew to the dot. Repeat for the other three dress-to-sleeve seams.

Hem the wrist end of the sleeves. Pin the dress at the sides, right sides together, again matching the dots. Sew one long seam from the wrist end of the sleeve, up to the dot, then down to the bottom of the skirt. (See Figure 2.) Repeat for the other side.

Cut from the neck to the dot on the *back side only* to make the neck opening. Turn the cut edges under and stitch. Next, turn the neck edge under and stitch it too. Gather the neckline to fit the doll, then add trim to secure the gathering.

Hem the bottom of the skirt and attach trim to the hem. Sew on a snap at the neck opening. If you wish, use a ribbon or make a sash from dress fabric to gather the dress at the waist.

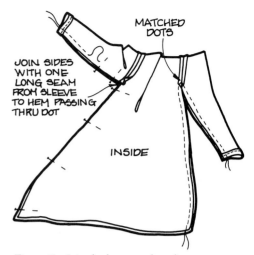

Figure 2. Join the bottom edge of each sleeve and the corresponding side of dress in one long seam.

11. Sew the apron. Turn the side hems and stitch them. Do the same with the bottom hem. Stitch the two seams on the bib and turn it inside out.

Gather the top edge of the apron to match dots with the sash. Center the bib on the back of the gathered apron, with the raw edges of the bib at the top of the apron. Stitch the bib to the apron. (See Figure 3.)

Fold the sash lengthwise. Stitch across the end and up the side, stopping at the dot. Repeat on the opposite side. Clip the seam to the dots and turn the sash inside out. Put one raw edge of the sash against the front of the gathered apron, matching the dots. You should have *three* raw edges together — bib, apron, and sash. Stitch again along the gathering, from dot to dot. Be careful not to catch the other side of the sash as you sew.

When you've finished, slip all the raw edges into the sash opening. Hand-stitch the opening closed. Turn the bib up and tack it to the top edge of the sash. (See Figure 4.)

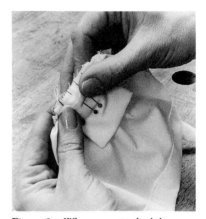

Figure 3. When you pin the bib to the apron, the raw (unturned) edge should face up.

12. Dress the doll. Slip the petticoat, the dress, and the apron on the doll. If you wish, glue a scrap of lace to the sides of the head to make a cap.

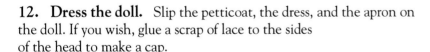

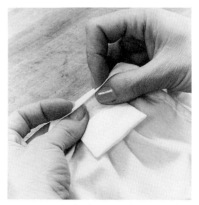

Figure 4. Hide the raw edges of the bib and the apron inside the sash.

COW SIGN

armers often hung hand-painted animal-shaped signs on their barns and outbuildings. They were usually advertisements, announcing a farmer's specialty to passersby. These signs were simple cutouts, shaped and painted to look like horses, cows, bulls, pigs, sheep, goats, geese, chickens, dogs — any farm or sporting animal. They also added a bit of fancy to otherwise plain, utilitarian buildings.

Livestock and dairy farmers used animal signs to publicize the type and breed of animal they raised. This rustic silhouette of a cow might have hung on a dairy barn, telling anyone interested that the resident dairyman milked a herd of Holstein cattle.

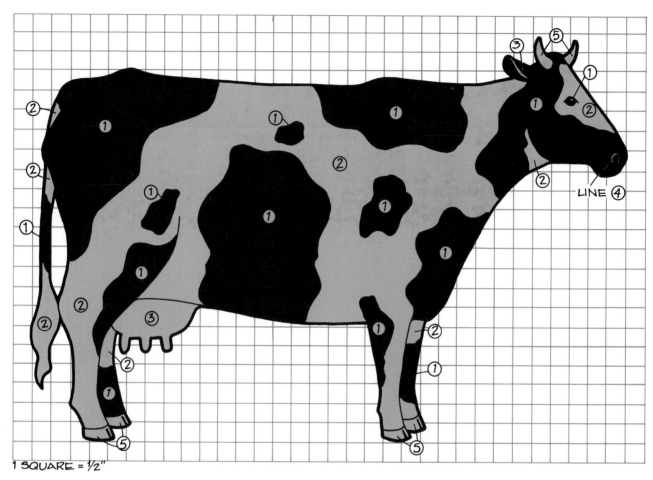

PATTERN

1 SQUARE = ½"

LINE

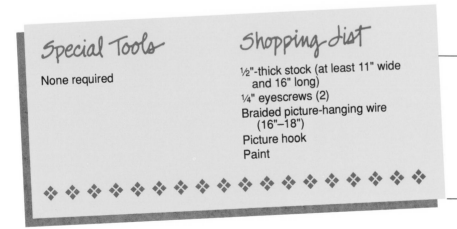

Special Tools

None required

Shopping List

½"-thick stock (at least 11" wide and 16" long)
¼" eyescrews (2)
Braided picture-hanging wire (16"–18")
Picture hook
Paint

CUTTING LIST

A. Cow sign   ½" x 11" x 16"

1. Choose the materials. Before you buy the stock for the cow sign, decide whether you want a sign that looks old and weathered or one that looks bright and new. Use solid lumber if you want the sign to look old. Most old-time barn signs were painted on solid wood, then hung outdoors. Over the years, the wood shrunk and cracked. You can duplicate this effect by using old barnwood to make your sign.

If you can't get old barnwood, use new lumber — preferably white pine or redwood. After you cut the shape of the sign, take it to a sandblasting service. Have them *lightly* blast the surface of the wood with fine sand or tiny glass beads. As the sand strikes the surface, it wears away the soft summer growth (light-colored wood) faster than the harder winter growth (darker annual rings). The surface becomes uneven, making the wood look old and weathered.

If you want the sign to look new, use commercial signboard or MDO-board. (The initials stand for "medium density overlay.") This outdoor plywood is covered on one side with paper to provide a smooth, even painting surface. The paper also protects the wood from the weather, if it's properly treated and finished. Signboard comes in 2' x 4', 4' x 4', and 4' x 8' sheets. It's available from most commercial lumberyards, although you may have to special-order it.

2. Cut the shape of the sign. Enlarge the cow pattern and transfer the pattern to the sign stock. Cut it out with a saber saw or a coping saw. Round over the edges with a file, then sand them to remove any tool marks.

3. Paint the sign. Color the cow shape, following the suggested color scheme or one of your own design. You may want to get a picture book of farm animals from the library to use as a color guide.

For a new-looking sign, apply the paint normally. To imitate a weathered look, apply the paint with what artists call a "dry brush." When you dip the brush in a color, load just a little paint on the tip. Wipe most of this off on paper or scrap wood. This makes the brush "dry." Apply what little remains to the sign. This technique lets you apply a very thin coat of color. Done properly, the finished piece looks as if most of the paint has weathered away. If you get the paint on too thick in any one spot, wipe it off with a damp cloth.

4. Hang the sign. Install two eyescrews in the back, near the top edge, on opposite sides. Stretch picture-hanging wire between them, then hang the sign from a picture hook.

Colors Shown:
① SOFT BLACK
② OFF WHITE
③ EQUAL PARTS OFF WHITE AND PEACHES N' CREAM
④ EQUAL PARTS RAW UMBER AND ANTIQUE WHITE
⑤ USE #4 MIXTURE, ADD 2 ADDITIONAL PARTS ANTIQUE WHITE

KEEPING BOX

Life on a pioneer farm was hard; you found your pleasures where you could. Country folk often seized even the smallest opportunity to fill their lives with color and gaiety.

The keeping box was a good example. Early American households used boxes of many sizes and shapes for storage. Sometimes a family member would make a small, rainbow-colored box to keep his or her personal treasures. These were called, appropriately enough, keeping boxes.

Keeping boxes were constructed very simply. However, the makers intricately decorated the outside of the boxes to attest to the value of the things inside. Occasionally they carved, inlaid, or laced the surfaces with moldings. Most often, they painted the boxes with geometric patterns and bright colors. The box you see here was patterned after a painted keeping box in the Winterthur Museum, near Wilmington, Delaware.

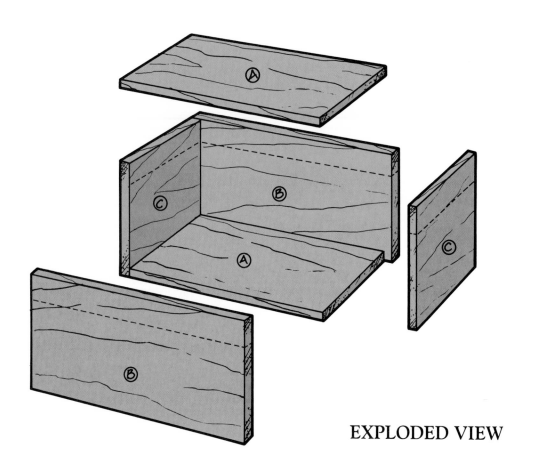

EXPLODED VIEW

Special Tools

Bar clamps (useful, but not absolutely necessary)

Shopping List

½"-thick plywood (at least 5¾" wide and 17" long)

½"-thick stock (at least 5" wide and 32" long)

Small brass butterfly hinges and mounting screws

Small brass clasp

1" wire brads

Carpenter's (yellow) glue

Paint

CUTTING LIST

A. Top/bottom (2) ½" x 5¾" x 8"
B. Front/back (2)   ½" x 5⅛" x 9"
C. Sides (2)   ½" x 5⅛" x 5¾"

1. Choose the materials. You can make the front, back, and sides from almost any wood, but use plywood for the top and bottom. This is more stable than solid wood — it doesn't expand and contract with changes in temperature and humidity. If you use solid wood for the top and bottom, they may expand enough to pop the corner joints — and ruin your project.

❖

2. Cut the parts to size. Cut the top, bottom, front, back, and sides to the dimensions in the Cutting List. Although the drawings show the box as 5" tall, make the front, back, and sides an extra 1/8" taller, as specified. When you cut the top off the box, you'll lose this 1/8". (The kerf — or width of the cut — of the average saw is 1/8".) When you put the lid back on the box, it will be 5" tall.

❖

3. Assemble the box. Finish-sand the faces of the wooden parts. Glue the top, bottom, back, front, and sides together, reinforcing the joints with 1"-long wire brads. With a wet rag, wipe off the glue that squeezes out of the joints. Let the remaining glue dry completely, then sand the joints clean and flush.

❖

4. Cut the lid from the box. Carefully draw a straight line 1" down from the top of the box, all around the front, back, and sides. Clamp the box to your workbench. Saw it in two at the line, using a handsaw. (See Figure 1.) Cut slowly, carefully following the line. After you cut the lid free, sand the sawed edges. (See Figure 2.)

❖

Figure 1. Instead of making the lid and the box separately, make them as one unit and cut them apart. This way, the lid will fit the box precisely.

Figure 2. To sand the sawed edges of the lid and the box, staple a sheet of sandpaper to a wide, flat board. Rub the lid and the box back and forth on the paper.

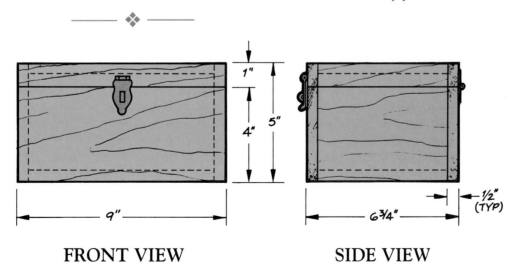

FRONT VIEW   **SIDE VIEW**

5. Hinge the lid to the box. Fit the lid to the box. Tape the two pieces together so they won't move or shift. Screw hinges to the back of the project, attaching the lid to the box. Screw a clasp to the front, to keep the lid closed.

Remove the tape and check the action of the hinges and the clasp. The box should open and close easily. When it's closed, the front, back, and sides should all be flush.

———— ❖ ————

6. Paint the box. Remove the lid from the box. Also remove the hinges and clasp from the lid. Set the hardware aside and lightly sand the wooden surfaces clean.

Enlarge the Top Pattern and the Front, Back, and Side Pattern. Trace the patterns on the top, front, back, and sides. The design for the front, back, and sides repeats, as shown in the drawing. Trace three tulips on each of the sides, and four on the front and back. Leave the bottom plain.

Paint the keeping box as suggested, or use your own color scheme. Paint the bottom, the inside of the box, and the inside of the lid a single color to complement the design on the other surfaces. When the paint dries, screw the hinge and the clasp back to the lid, and attach the lid to the box.

———— ❖ ————

TOP PATTERN
(HALF SIZE)

Colors Shown:

BACKGROUND — EQUAL PARTS PINE NEEDLE GREEN AND TELEMARK GREEN

TULIPS — EQUAL PARTS JOSONJA RED AND L'ORANGERIE

LINES IN TULIPS — JOSONJA RED

HEART — ONE PART L'ORANGERIE AND TWO PARTS JOSONJA RED

TULIP LEAVES — EQUAL PARTS GREEN OLIVE AND MUSHROOM

LINES IN TULIP LEAVES — GREEN OLIVE

VINES — ONE PART GREEN OLIVE AND TWO PARTS ANTIQUE WHITE

BERRIES, BACKGROUND AROUND HEART, DOTS ALONG TULIP STEMS — OFF WHITE

CHECKERS — ANTIQUE WHITE AND VILLAGE GREEN

EDGING, STRIPES DIVIDING AREAS — EQUAL PARTS VILLAGE GREEN AND ANTIQUE WHITE

STARBURSTS ON TOP AND SIDES — ANTIQUE WHITE

DIAGONAL STRIPES AND DOTS ON SIDE BORDERS — VILLAGE GREEN

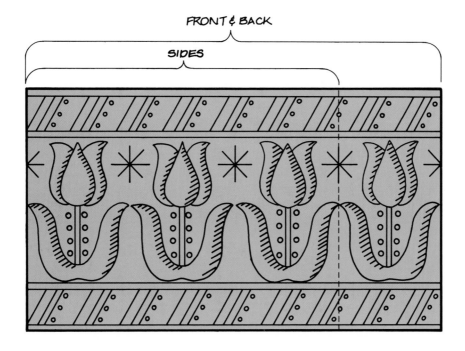

FRONT, BACK, AND SIDES
(HALF SIZE)

POUTING CHAIR

t's really not a chair. It's a stepstool with a tall handle. Country folk made these high-back stools for their kitchens, to help them reach the high shelves in the pantry and cupboards. The handle lets them move the stool around easily, without having to bend over to pick it up.

When not being used, the stool was kept in an out-of-the-way corner — probably the same corner where naughty children were banished from time to time. The children would sit on the stool while they contemplated their misdeeds. Consequently, a high-back stool became whimsically known as a pouting chair.

The chair was constructed from several flat boards, glued and screwed together. The back leg was extended to make the handle, which was often decorated. The handle on the pouting chair you see here is carved and painted with a heart nested in teardrops — a fitting design for a pouting chair.

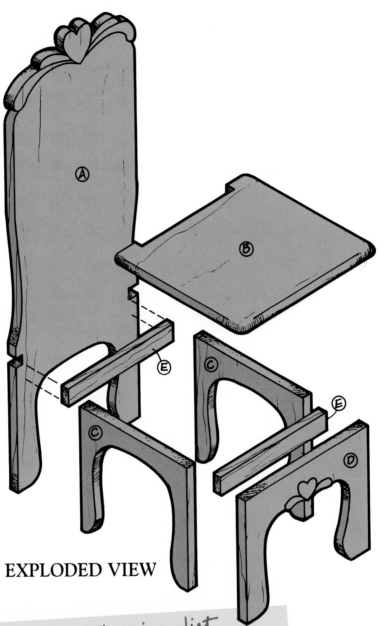

EXPLODED VIEW

Special Tools

Bench knife, to carve the design

Shopping List

¾"-thick stock (a 1 x 12, at least
    90" long)
#10 x 1¼" flathead wood screws
    (20–24)
⅜"-diameter dowel (at least
    12" long)
Carpenter's (yellow) glue
Paint

CUTTING LIST

A.	Back	¾" x 11" x 36"
B.	Seat	¾" x 11¼" x 12"
C.	Side legs (2)	¾" x 9¼" x 9¼"
D.	Front legs	¾" x 9¼" x 11"
E.	Ledgers (2)	¾" x 2" x 9½"

1. Choose the materials. Make this project from a wood that's both light and strong. The stool must support your weight when you stand on it, but it should also be light enough to lift easily. White and yellow pine are the best choices.

———— ❖ ————

2. Cut the parts to size and shape. Cut the wooden parts to the dimensions in the Cutting List. Enlarge the Front Legs Pattern, Side Legs Pattern, and Back Pattern. Trace the patterns on the stock. Also lay out the notch on the back edge of the seat, as shown in the Seat Layout.

Before you cut the parts, double-check the measurements and positions of the notches in the back. When you cut the notch in the seat, you'll create a short tenon on either side of the seat. These tenons must fit in the back notches. To fit properly, those notches must be *precisely* 9¼" from the bottom edge. They should also be ¾" wide, ¾" deep, and 9½" apart as measured from the inside edge of one notch to the inside edge of the other.

When you're satisfied that you have positioned the notches properly, cut the shapes of the back, seat, side legs, and front legs. Use a saber saw or a coping saw. When making the straight sides of the notches, cut very slowly. Be careful that the blade doesn't wander from the line. After cutting, sand the curved edges. It's not necessary to sand the straight sides of the notches.

———— ❖ ————

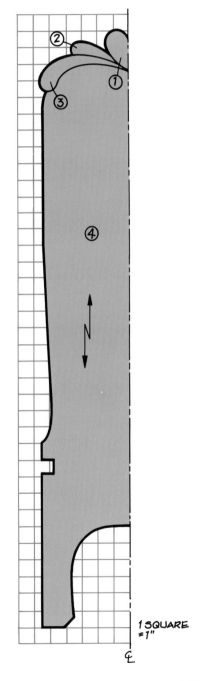

Colors Shown:
- ① APACHE RED
- ② PRAIRIE GREEN
- ③ INDIAN SKY
- ④ EQUAL PARTS SOLDIER BLUE AND OFF WHITE

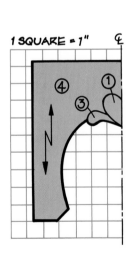

FRONT LEGS PATTERN

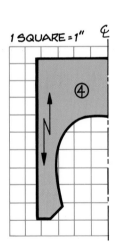

SIDE LEGS PATTERN
(Cut 2)

BACK PATTERN

Figure 1. With the bench knife, cut the outline of the heart and teardrop shapes. Slice straight down, about ⅛" deep.

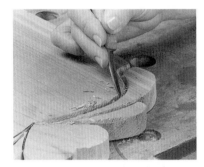

Figure 2. After you outline the shapes, hold the knife at an angle and pare away some of the stock that surrounds them. Make the surface of the wood slope in toward the shapes. Outline the shapes again, and pare away some more of the surrounding stock. Repeat until the heart and teardrops seem to stand out about ¼" from the stock.

Figure 3. Shave the edges of the heart and teardrop shapes with the knife. Remove tiny amounts of stock at different angles until the edges are rounded over. Don't remove too much stock or the shapes will look flat and poorly defined. Remove just enough to soften the hard edges.

3. Carve the shapes of the hearts and teardrops. The hearts and teardrops on the back and the front legs are carved very slightly to make them stand out from the surface. This is not difficult; it requires no carving experience — just a little patience.

Start by slicing along the pattern line with a bench knife. Cut straight down, about ⅛" deep. (See Figure 1.) Then remove stock around the outside of the hearts and teardrops. Make these cuts at a shallow angle, so the stock seems to slope down to the edge of the heart. (See Figure 2.) Repeat the first and second cuts, making the shapes stand out about ¼" from the stock. Finally, round the edges of the shapes. (See Figure 3.) Sand the carvings to remove any knife marks.

Tip: Sharpen your bench knife carefully before you start carving. As you work, whet the edge occasionally to keep it sharp. The sharper the knife, the easier it is to carve the wood.

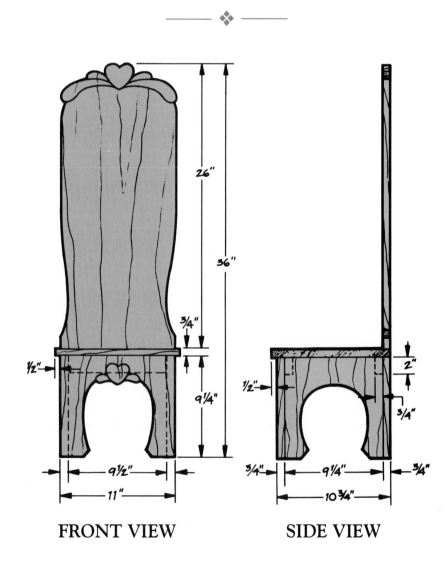

FRONT VIEW   **SIDE VIEW**

4. Assemble the pouting chair. Finish-sand the surfaces of all the parts. Fasten the ledgers to the back and the front legs. On the back, position the top edge of the ledger flush with the bottom edges of the notches. On the front legs, make the top edges of both parts flush. Center the ledgers between the sides. Don't glue them in place, just drive screws through the ledgers and into the other parts. Use a screw drill to countersink the heads of the screws.

Note: The grain direction of the ledgers runs perpendicular to the other parts. Because wood expands and contracts across the grain, a ledger will keep another part from expanding and contracting evenly if it's glued in place. That part will warp or split, ruining the chair. The screws, however, bend slightly as the wood moves.

Assemble the remaining parts with glue *and* screws. Use the screw drill to counterbore and countersink the screw heads. The counterbores should be approximately ¼" deep, so the heads will rest below the surface. With a coping saw, cut the ⅜"-diameter dowel into ⅜"-long plugs. Dip these plugs in glue and press them into the counterbores, covering the screw heads. (See Figure 4.)

With a wet rag, wipe off any excess glue that squeezes out of the joints and around the plugs. Let the remaining glue dry, then sand the joints clean and flush. File and sand the plugs even with the wood surface, as shown in the Screw Joinery Detail. (See Figure 5.)

Figure 4. To hide the screw heads, glue dowel plugs in the counterbores.

Figure 5. After the glue dries, file or sand the plugs flush to the surface of the wood. The chair will look as if you pegged it together.

❖

5. Paint the chair. Lightly sand all the wooden surfaces to clean them. Paint the chair as suggested, or devise your own color scheme. You can also stain and finish the chair, if you'd rather have a natural wood look.

❖

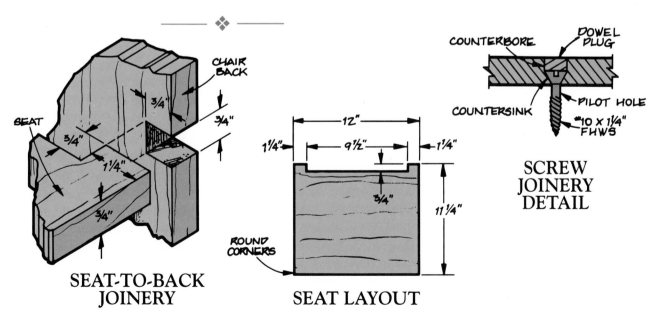

SEAT-TO-BACK JOINERY

SEAT LAYOUT

SCREW JOINERY DETAIL

WOOLLY SHEEP

ountry folks often made figurines just to exercise their creativity and cleverness. Sometimes they used unorthodox materials, particularly when that material reminded them of a person or animal. A dried apple could be the wrinkled countenance of an old woman, a pine cone made to resemble a hedgehog, a handful of clothespins transformed into a whole miniature family. And wood shavings? A woolly sheep, of course.

At the heart of this figurine is a block of soft wood, shaped to resemble the body and head of a sheep. Dowels represent the legs and ears. The block is covered with hundreds of paper-thin, curly wood shavings — the by-product of a bench plane. Presto! A woolly sheep.

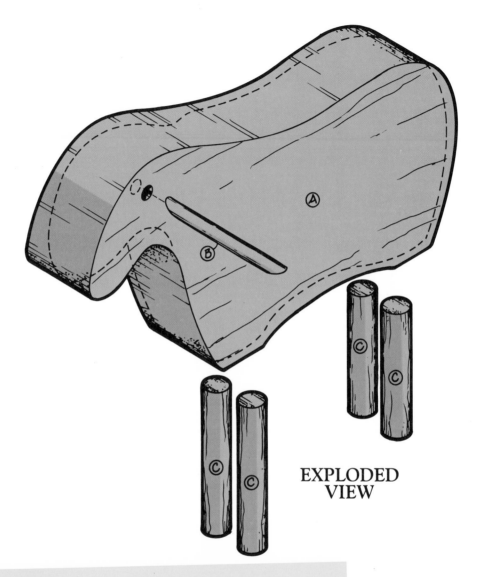

EXPLODED
VIEW

CUTTING LIST

A. Body   1½" x 4¾" x 8½"
B. Ears   ¼"-diameter x 2¾"
C. Legs (4) ½"-diameter x 2¾"

1. Choose the materials. To shape the sheep's body, you must do a little woodcarving. To make this carving easier, select a soft wood. The easiest wood to carve is basswood, which is available at many hobby stores and most lumberyards that carry hardwoods. If you can't get basswood, clear white pine is a good second choice.

You'll also need some scrap wood to make the fleece. Any wood can be used, but it should be as light as possible, so the fleece appears white. Poplar, pine, maple, basswood, and birch will all do well.

Colors Shown:

FACE, EARS AND LEGS —
SOFT BLACK

❖

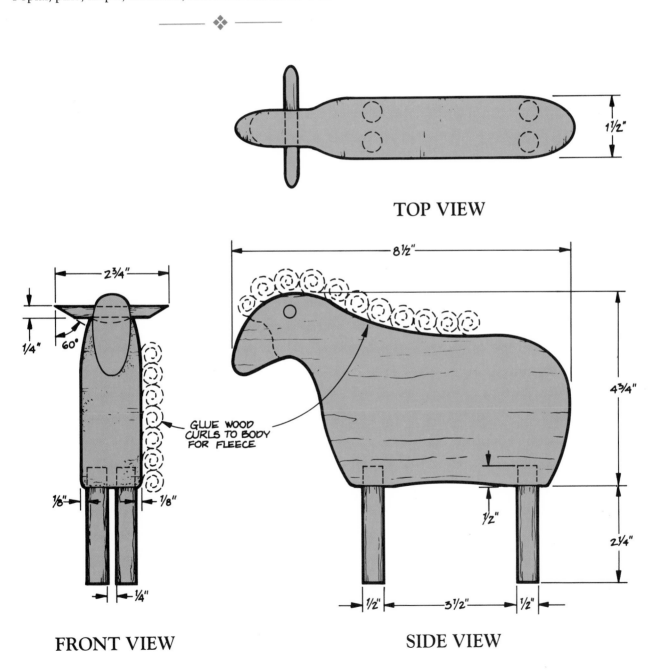

TOP VIEW

GLUE WOOD
CURLS TO BODY
FOR FLEECE

FRONT VIEW

SIDE VIEW

WOOLLY SHEEP   151

Figure 1. Clamp the body to your workbench to drill it. Wrap a piece of masking tape around the drill bit to gauge the depth of the hole.

2. Cut the parts to size. Using a handsaw, cut the 1½"-thick block slightly larger than the length and width shown in the Cutting List. This will give you some extra room to saw the shape of the sheep. Cut the leg and ear dowels with a coping saw. Miter the ends of the ear dowel at 60°, as shown in the Front View.

3. Cut the shape of the body. Enlarge the Sheep Pattern and trace it onto the stock. Be sure to trace the entire pattern, including the lines that indicate the location of the leg and ear holes. Cut the shape of the body with a saber saw or coping saw, then sand the edges to remove the saw marks.

4. Drill the leg and ear holes. Drill a ¼"-diameter hole through the sheep's head, where you want to place the ear dowel. Then drill holes ½" in diameter and ½" deep in the bottom surface of the body to mount the leg dowels. To keep from making these holes too deep, wrap a piece of masking tape around the bit, ½" from the end. When you bore the holes, stop the drill when the tape is even with the surface of the wood. (See Figure 1.)

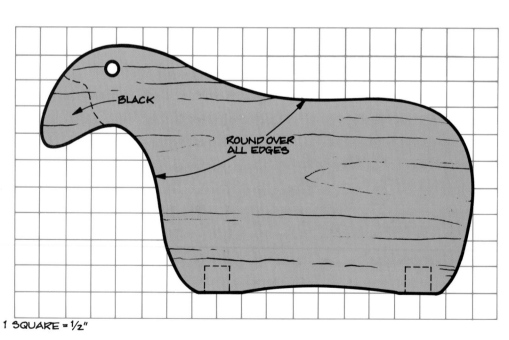

1 SQUARE = ½"

SHEEP PATTERN

5. Carve the sheep's body. Once the body has been sawed and drilled, it must be carved to look like a sheep. The shoulders, withers, and other edges must be rounded, as shown in the Front View. The head should be narrowed slightly, as shown in the Top View. This doesn't require any special carving skills, but it does take time and patience.

Use a bench or carving knife to shape the body. Remove just a bit of wood at a time, until you get the shape you want. As you work, pay attention to the direction of the wood grain. If the knife wants to dig in, you're probably cutting into the grain, or "uphill," as some carvers call it. Turn the piece so you always cut away from the grain, or "downhill." (See Figure 2.) When you have carved the body to its rough shape, sand the surface to remove the chisel marks.

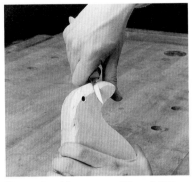

Figure 2. Always carve "downhill," away from the grain. If the knife wants to dig in when you carve, turn the wood around.

6. Assemble the body, ears, and legs. Glue the ear dowel in the head, with the mitered ends facing down, as shown in the Front View. Center the ears so they stick out an equal distance on each side. Also, glue the legs in their mounting holes. Before the glue dries, set the sheep on a table and straighten the legs. With a wet rag, wipe away any glue that squeezes out of the holes.

Figure 3. To make the fleece, shave a scrap of wood with a bench plane. This process will be much easier if you shave an *edge* of the board, rather than the face or end.

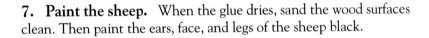

7. Paint the sheep. When the glue dries, sand the wood surfaces clean. Then paint the ears, face, and legs of the sheep black.

8. Make and attach the fleece. Make the fleece for the sheep by shaving a scrap board with a bench plane. Adjust the plane's blade to shave very thin strips of wood — the thinner the strips, the more they'll curl. Clamp the board to your workbench, then push the plane across the edge with long, even strokes. The wood will peel off in tightly curled strips. (See Figure 3.) Stop when you have about two cups of curls.

Carefully glue the wood curls to the sheep's body, starting at the back end and working your way forward. Apply a dab of glue to each curl, position it on the sheep, and hold it in place with a pushpin. (See Figure 4.) Cover the entire sheep, except the face, ears, and legs.

Figure 4. Glue ten to fifteen curls to the sheep at one time, holding them in place with pushpins. Let the glue dry, remove the pins, and glue another set. Place the curls as close as possible, so you can't see the surface of the sheep.

MANTEL CLOCK ❖

he American mantel clock was once a common sight in every country home — not only on this continent, but in South America, Europe, and parts of Asia as well. This sawed-off version of the English grandfather clock was perhaps the first mass-produced household appliance, an early triumph of American ingenuity.

In the early nineteenth century, several New England clockmakers adapted new woodworking and metalworking machines to increase their production. At the same time, they experimented with a revolutionary new production method: the assembly line. The result was an abundance of inexpensive, reliable clocks. For the first time, common folks all over the world could afford a timepiece of their own. For most of the century, American clockmakers exported their distinctive "mantel clocks" to every part of the globe.

The clock shown is typical of nineteenth-century mantel clocks. The case is a simple box with two compartments — one for the clock face and the other for the pendulum. The frame surrounding the face is painted in the traditional American primitive style. The pendulum swings and the clockworks tick, just like the genuine article. Only by looking inside can you tell this is a product of the twentieth century — the movement is an inexpensive battery-run quartz clock. This simplifies the project without detracting from its country charm.

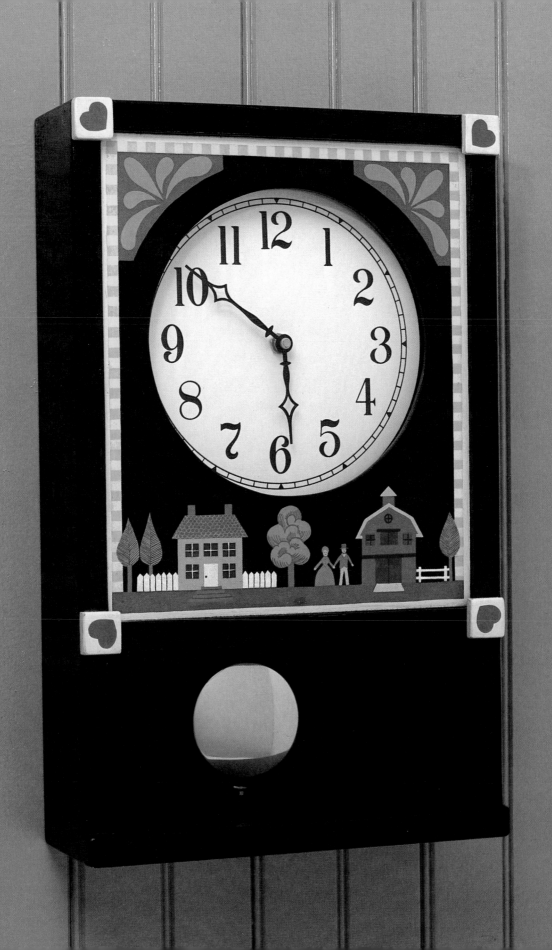

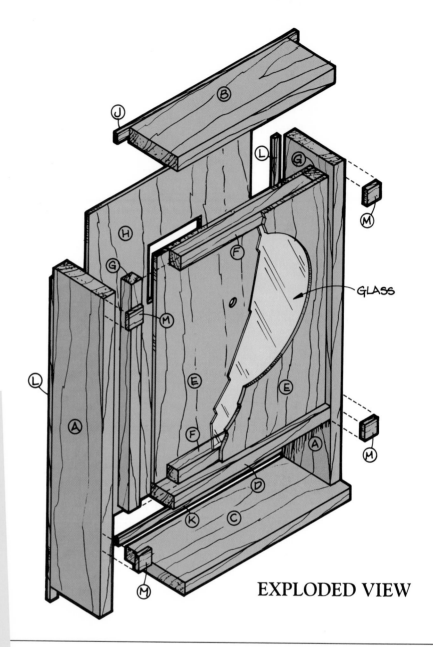

GLASS

EXPLODED VIEW

Special Tools

Backsaw, to cut the ledgers and ornaments
Miter box, to guide the backsaw

Shopping List

¾"-thick stock (at least 11" wide and 48" long)
¼"-thick stock (at least 11" wide and 30" long)
¼"-thick hardboard (approximately 2' x 2')
8" printed clockface (paper or sheet metal)
Quartz movement with 12" pendulum
3½" clock hands (minute and hour)
4d finishing nails (20–24)
¾" wire brads
#6 x ¾" roundhead wood screws (4)
Plate glass (⅛" x 8⅝" x 11⅞")
Glazing points (4–6)
Carpenter's (yellow) glue
Contact cement
Paint

❖ ❖ ❖ ❖ ❖ ❖ ❖ ❖ ❖

CUTTING LIST

A.	Sides (2)	¾" x 3¼" x 18⅜"
B.	Top	¾" x 3¼" x 10¼"
C.	Bottom	¾" x 4" x 11¾"
D.	Shelf	¾" x 1½" x 10¼"
E.	Front/mounting boards (2)	¼" x 10¼" x 13½"
F.	Top/bottom spacers (2)	¾" x ¾" x 8¾"

G.	Side spacers (2)	¾" x ¾" x 13½"
H.	Back	¼" x 10¾" x 18⅛"
J.	Top ledger	¼" x ½" x 11¾"
K.	Bottom ledger	¼" x ½" x 10¾"
L.	Side ledgers (2)	¼" x ½" x 18⅝"
M.	Ornaments (4)	¼" x ⅞" x ⅞"

1. Choose the materials. If you plan to paint the clock as shown, you can make the case from almost any wood. If you stain it, white pine, maple, and birch all take a stain well. If you want a natural finish, use a hardwood with an interesting grain pattern. Individual clockmakers often used cherry or walnut; clock manufacturers preferred oak. Whatever wood you choose, make both the ¼"- and ¾"-thick wooden parts from the *same* species. If you use different woods, the glue joints between the sides, side ledgers, front, and ornaments will be plainly visible even if you paint the case.

Make the mounting board and the clock back from hardboard (sometimes referred to as Masonite™). If the yardman asks whether you want tempered or untempered hardboard, choose tempered. It cuts easier and lasts longer.

Purchase the clock movement, pendulum, face, and hands from a clockmaking supplier. (See Appendix B for addresses.) Before you order, there are several things you should know:

■ Not all movements are the same size. Check that the movement you order will fit the case.

■ The length of the pendulum is traditionally measured from the center of the hand shaft on the movement to the tip of the pendulum, even though the actual pendulum isn't quite this long. Order a movement with a 12" pendulum.

■ The actual size of the time ring on a clockface will be somewhat smaller than the diameter of the dial. Order an 8" dial with a 7" time ring. Choose something plain, preferably a white background with simple black lettering. Most mantel clocks had plain faces and decorated cases.

■ The size of the hands is measured by the length of the minute hand, even though the hour hand will be somewhat shorter. Order a set of 3½" hands. Don't bother to order a second hand — few nineteenth-century clocks had these.

Figure 1. Use the 90° slot on a miter box to cut the ledgers and the ornaments. This insures that the ends are perfectly square.

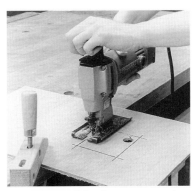

Figure 2. To make the openings in the front and back, you must drill a starting hole first, then saw outward from this hole, cutting the shape of the opening. This technique is called piercing.

❖

2. Cut the parts to size. Cut all the wooden and hardboard parts to the sizes in the Cutting List. To make the ledger and the ornaments, first rip ¼"-thick stock to the proper width with a handsaw. Then, using a miter box and a backsaw, cut the parts to length. (See Figure 1.)

❖

3. Cut openings in the front and back. Both the front and back must have openings cut in them. The front opening allows you to see the clock face, while the back opening lets you reach the movement to set the time or to change the batteries.

To make each opening, mark its outline on the stock. For the front opening, draw a 7¾"-diameter circle as shown in the Front View. For back opening, mark a rectangle about ½" taller and wider than the clock movement. Position this rectangle so it will be even with the movement when you assemble the case, as shown in Section A. Drill a ¾"-diameter hole through the waste, inside the outline of each opening. Insert the blade of a saber saw or coping saw through the hole, and cut to the outline. Continue cutting, following the outline, until the waste is free. Sand the edges of the opening to remove the saw marks. (See Figure 2.)

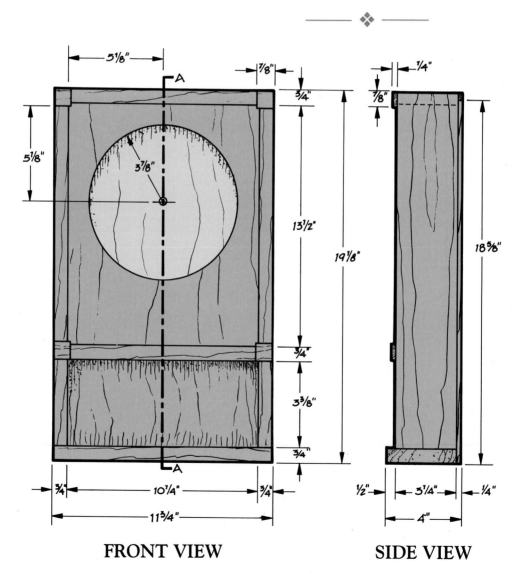

FRONT VIEW   **SIDE VIEW**

4. Drill a mounting hole for the movement. The movement is attached to the mounting board by the threaded hand shaft. Measure the diameter of this hand shaft (most will be ⅜"–½" in diameter), and drill a hole through the mounting board. Insert the hand shaft through the hole to test its fit, but don't mount it to the board yet.

Important Note: The hand shaft hole must be centered on the mounting board in *precisely* the same position you centered the circular opening in the front: 5⅛" in from one side and 5⅛" down from the top. Otherwise, the clock face will not be properly centered in the opening.

❖

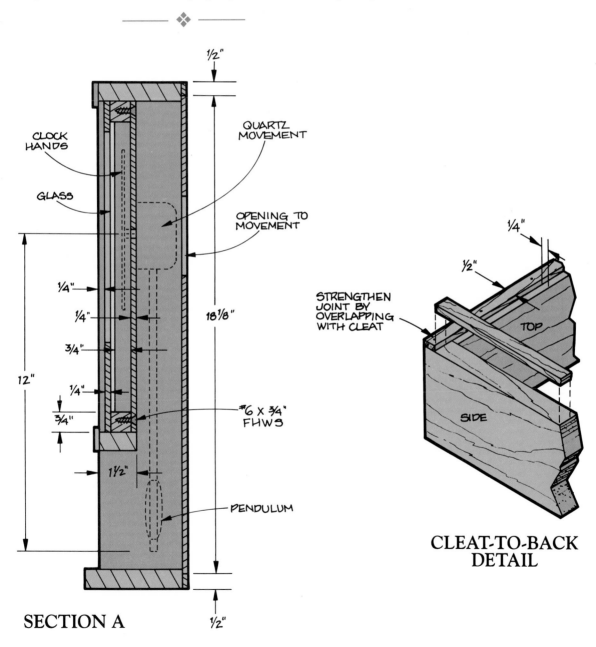

SECTION A

CLEAT-TO-BACK
DETAIL

Figure 3. Glazing points are specially made to keep glass in place in a frame. Push the points into the wood with the tip of a screwdriver, as shown.

Figure 4. The clock movement is held in place with a single nut on the hand shaft. Tighten this nut with pliers, being careful not to get it *too* tight. You don't want to twist the hand shaft out of the movement.

5. Assemble the clock case. Finish-sand all wooden parts. Be careful not to round over any of the adjoining ends or edges as you sand.

Glue the top, shelf, and sides together, reinforcing the glue joints with finishing nails. Then attach the bottom and the spacers with glue and nails. Finally, attach the front, ledgers, and ornaments. Join these ¼"-thick parts with glue and wire brads. With a wet rag, wipe away any excess glue that squeezes out of the joints.

After the glue dries, carefully sand the outside edges of the ledgers flush with the faces of the top and sides. Using a nail punch, set the heads of the nails and brads below the surface of the wood.

6. Paint or finish the clock case. Do any necessary touch-up sanding on the assembled case. Then apply a stain, finish, or paint, as you wish.

If you choose to paint the case, enlarge the Front Pattern and trace it on the front. Paint the front as suggested, or use your own color scheme. Also paint the outside of the case, the inside of the compartment under the shelf, and the front face of the back. Make these a single, solid color to complement the design on the front.

7. Mount the clock movement in the case. Carefully clean the glass, then insert it between the spacers, against the inside surface of the front. Secure it by driving glazing points into the spacers. (See Figure 3.)

Using contact cement, mount the clock face on the front surface of the mounting board. Carefully center the hole in the face over the hand shaft hole in the board. Insert the hand shaft through the hole and turn the movement so the pendulum hanger points down. Put a washer over the hand shaft to protect the clock face. Then put a nut on the hand shaft and tighten it down to secure the movement. (See Figure 4.)

Press the clock hands onto the shaft and put the small cap nut on the minute hand shaft. (This cap nut usually comes with the movement.) Turn the time-set knob on the back of the movement so the minute hand points to 12 o'clock, then *push* the hour hand with your finger so it also points to 12. Place the mounting board between the spacers and secure it with small roundhead wood screws.

Attach the pendulum to the movement. Put a battery in the clock, set the time, and start the pendulum swinging to make sure it doesn't hit or rub against any part of the case. Let the clock run for several days to see if it keeps proper time. If it loses or gains time, adjust the position of the bob on the pendulum according to the manufacturer's directions.

When you're satisfied the clock keeps good time, place the back between the ledgers. Secure it to the case with wire brads, but *don't* glue it. You may need to remove the back in the future.

FRONT
PATTERN
(HALF SIZE)

⑦ LINES ON PINE TREES
⑳ LINES ON OAK TREE
⑰ LINES ON HOUSE ROOF

FLESH

Colors Shown:

① SOFT BLACK
② EQUAL PARTS BARN RED AND SUNKISS YELLOW
③ EQUAL PARTS CACTUS FLOWER AND OFF WHITE
④ EQUAL PARTS SUNKISS YELLOW AND CACTUS FLOWER
⑤ EQUAL PARTS SUNKISS YELLOW AND DIJON GOLD
⑥ GREEN OLIVE

⑦ GREEN APPLE
⑧ EQUAL PARTS GREEN APPLE AND VILLAGE GREEN
⑨ OFF WHITE
⑩ EQUAL PARTS SOFT BLUE AND SOFT GRAY
⑪ EQUAL PARTS MONET BLUE AND STONEWARE BLUE
⑫ SOLDIER BLUE
⑬ SEDONA CLAY
⑭ EQUAL PARTS BORDEAUX AND SEDONA CLAY

⑮ EQUAL PARTS BORDEAUX AND BARN RED
⑯ EQUAL PARTS SOFT GRAY AND INDIAN SKY
⑰ EQUAL PARTS SOLDIER BLUE AND STONEWARE BLUE
⑱ FLESH
⑲ ROSEBERRY
⑳ CHATEAU MOSS
㉑ STONEWARE BLUE

ANIMAL PULL TOYS

**P**ull toys have been around since ancient times. Archaeologists have found small carvings of animals, mounted on wheels, in Egyptian tombs. But up until the last few centuries, these were rare, usually reserved for the children of the rich and powerful. Most common playthings were ordinary miniatures.

In the beginning of the last century, however, the Industrial Revolution created a new interest in locomotion. It also helped to create a toy industry. Before long, playthings that moved or rolled became commonplace.

These pull toys are typical of many in the nineteenth century. Animals have always fascinated children, so parents bought or made moving animals of all sorts — farm animals, circus animals, and household pets — for their children. Shown are three farm animals — a pig, a horse, and a family of ducks.

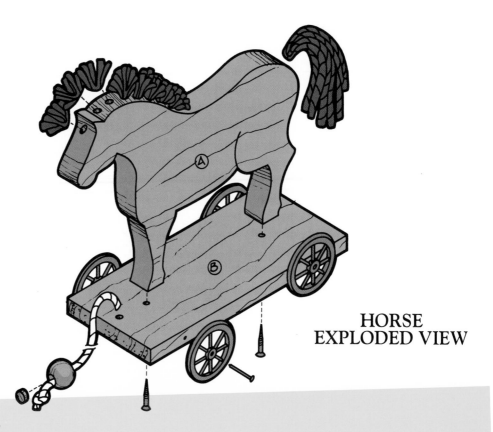

**HORSE
EXPLODED VIEW**

None required

Shopping List

Horse
¾"-thick stock (1 board, at least
  7" x 8½")
½"-thick stock (1 board, at
  least 3" x 7")
1"-diameter wooden bead
½"-diameter dowel (at least
  1" long)
³⁄₁₆"-diameter nylon rope (24")
1½"-diameter metal wheels and
  axle nails (4)
#8 x 1¼" flathead wood
  screws (2)
Carpenter's (yellow) glue
Paint

Pig
¾"-thick stock (1 board, at least
  4" x 6")
½"-thick stock (1 board, at least
  3" x 6")
1"-diameter wooden bead
½"-diameter dowel (at least
  1" long)
³⁄₁₆"-diameter nylon rope (24")
1½"-diameter metal wheels and
  axle nails (4)
#8 x 1¼" flathead wood
  screws (2)
Carpenter's (yellow) glue
Paint

Mother Duck and Ducklings
¾"-thick stock (1 board, at least
  5" x 12")
½"-thick stock (1 board, at least
  3" x 18")
¼"-thick stock (1 board, at least
  1½" x 6")
1"-diameter wooden bead
³⁄₁₆"-diameter nylon rope (42")
1½"-diameter metal wheels and
  axle nails (4)
1"-diameter metal wheels and
  axle nails (12)
½"-diameter dowel (at least
  1" long)
¼"-diameter dowel (at least
  4" long)
³⁄₁₆"-diameter dowel (at least
  8" long)
Carpenter's (yellow) glue
Paint

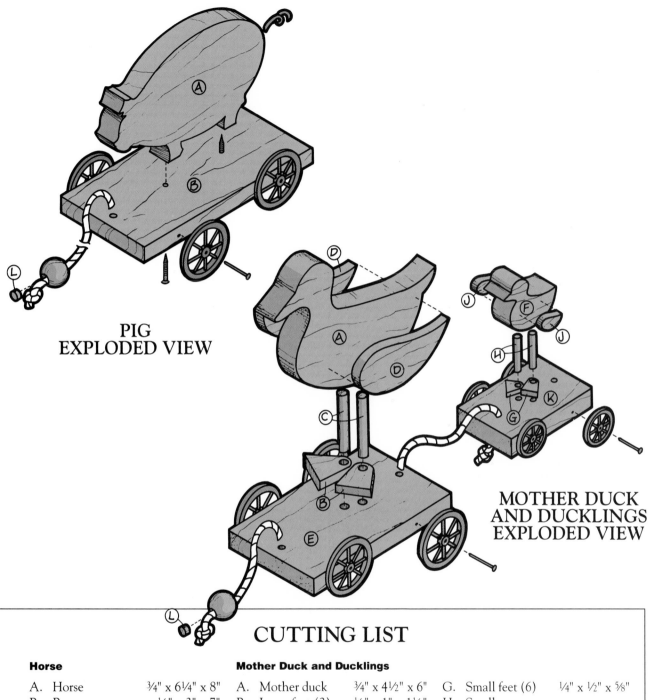

PIG
EXPLODED VIEW

MOTHER DUCK
AND DUCKLINGS
EXPLODED VIEW

CUTTING LIST

Horse

A.	Horse	¾" x 6¼" x 8"
B.	Base	½" x 3" x 7"
C.	Plug	½" diameter x ¼"

Pig

A.	Pig	¾" x 3½" x 5½"
B.	Base	½" x 3" x 6"
C.	Plug	½" diameter x ¼"

Mother Duck and Ducklings

A.	Mother duck	¾" x 4½" x 6"
B.	Large feet (2)	¼" x 1" x 1¼"
C.	Large legs (2)	¼" diameter x 1¾"
D.	Large wings (2)	¼" x 1½" x 3¼"
E.	Large base	½" x 3" x 5"
F.	Ducklings (3)	¾" x 1¾" x 2⅛"

G.	Small feet (6)	¼" x ½" x ⅝"
H.	Small legs (6)	3⁄16" diameter x 1"
J.	Small wings (6)	¼" x ½" x ¾"
K.	Small bases (3)	½" x 2" x 3"
L.	Plug	½" diameter x ¼"

❖ Horse and Pig

1. Choose the materials. Pull toys can be made from almost any domestic hardwood. The ones shown are built of poplar, but you can also use cherry, maple, or oak. If you're making this pull toy for a child, avoid softwoods, such as pine and fir. Softwoods can't stand up to the abuse that children can deal out.

Purchase the wood from any lumberyard that carries hardwoods, and have the yardman plane the ¾"-, ½"-, and ¼"-thick stock you need. You can find wooden beads and metal wheels at most crafts and hobby stores, or you can buy them from a mail-order woodworking supply company. Refer to Appendix B for addresses.

❖

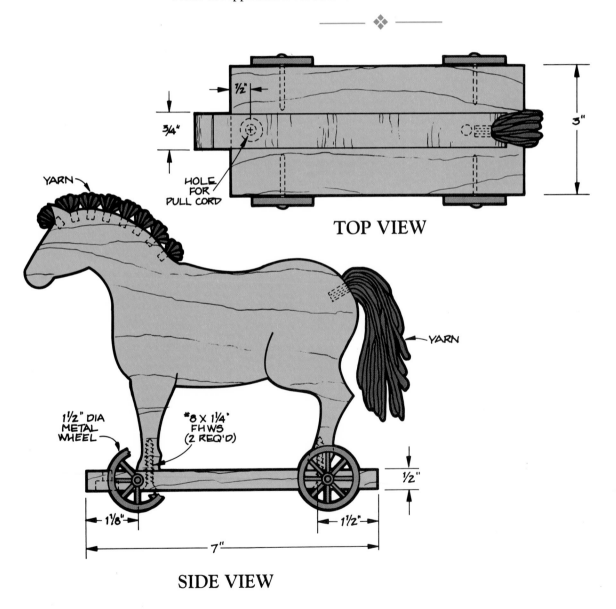

TOP VIEW

SIDE VIEW

2. Cut the wooden parts to size. Cut the animal's body and base to the sizes given in the Cutting List. (**Note:** Cut the body parts slightly oversize to give yourself a little extra room to cut the shapes.) Cut the plug from ½"-diameter dowel stock with a coping saw.

——— ❖ ———

3. Cut the shape of the body. Trace the Horse Pattern or Pig Pattern onto the wood. Cut out the shape with a saber saw or coping saw, then sand the edges smooth.

——— ❖ ———

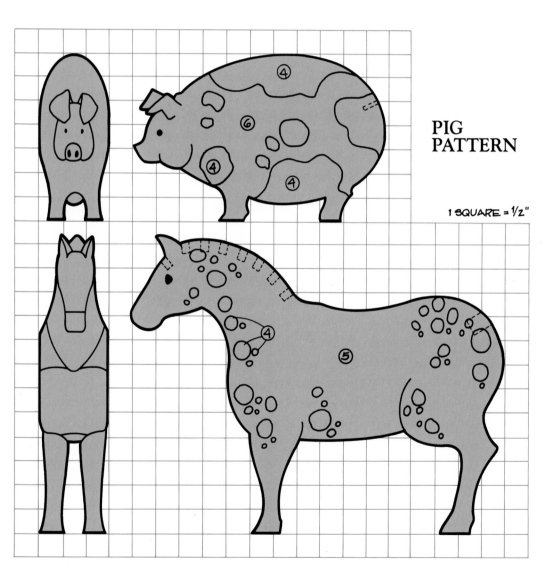

PIG PATTERN

1 SQUARE = ½"

SIDE PATTERN (FOR CARVING)   **HORSE PATTERN**

Figure 1. To keep the wooden bead from rolling around when you drill it, first drill a ⅞"-diameter hole in a scrap of wood. Place the bead in the hole, then drill the hole and recess in the bead.

4. Drill the holes in the base and bead. The pull cord attaches to the base and the bead through small holes. It's knotted, so it can't be pulled back through the holes. The knots sit in recesses, so you don't notice them. To make this hole and recess in the base, drill a ½"-diameter hole, ¼" deep in the bottom surface where you want to attach the pull cord. Then drill a ³⁄₁₆"-diameter hole in the center of the first one, through the base, as shown in the Holes for Pull Cord Detail. Make the hole and recess in the bead in the same manner, except drill the ½"-diameter hole ½" deep — halfway through the bead. (See Figure 1.)

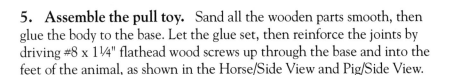

5. Assemble the pull toy. Sand all the wooden parts smooth, then glue the body to the base. Let the glue set, then reinforce the joints by driving #8 x 1¼" flathead wood screws up through the base and into the feet of the animal, as shown in the Horse/Side View and Pig/Side View.

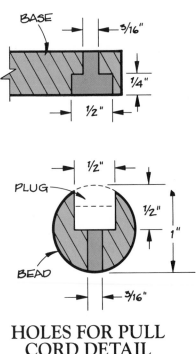

HOLES FOR PULL CORD DETAIL

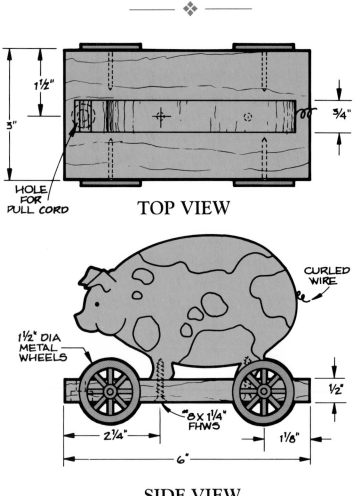

TOP VIEW

SIDE VIEW

6. Paint the pull toy. Round the edges with a file and sandpaper to remove any sharp corners. Sand the wooden surfaces clean, then paint the animal and base. Follow the suggested color scheme or invent your own.

——— ❖ ———

7. Attach the wheels, pull cord, and bead. Mount the wheels, driving the axle nails into the base. Tap the nails into the wood until the wheels are *almost* snug against the edge of the base. Each wheel must spin freely. If it doesn't, pry the nail out slightly.

Insert the end of the nylon rope through the 3⁄16"-diameter hole in the bead. Tie a knot in the end of the rope and pull it back through the hole, so the knot rests in the 1⁄2"-diameter recess. Glue the plug in the recess, covering the knot. When the glue dries, file the end of the plug flush with the bead. (See Figure 2.) Paint or apply a finish to the bead.

Insert the other end of the rope down through the 3⁄16"-diameter hole in the base. Tie a knot in the end, then nest it in the recess, as you did with the bead. Put a few drops of glue on the knot to keep it in the base recess.

Figure 2. Sand or file the plug to blend it with the surface of the bead. Try to make it follow the same round contour.

❖ Mother Duck and Ducklings

1. Choose the materials. To make the duck and ducklings, purchase a hardwood, such as poplar, cherry, maple, or birch, to stand up to use and abuse.

——— ❖ ———

2. Cut the wooden parts to size. Cut the duck's and duckling's bodies, feet, and wings to the sizes given in the Cutting List. Saw the legs and the plug from dowel stock with a coping saw.

——— ❖ ———

3. Cut the shapes of the bodies, feet, and wings. Trace the Duck and Duckling Patterns onto the wood. Cut out the shapes with a saber saw or coping saw, then sand the edges smooth.

——— ❖ ———

4. Drill the holes in the bases, bodies, feet, and bead. Drill holes for the pull cords in the bases and bead, in the same manner as described in step 4 for the horse and pig pull toys. However, make *two* sets of holes and recesses in the bases, so you can tie them together.

Figure 3. To locate the leg holes in the base for a duck or duckling, you must first drill the leg holes in the body. Insert the legs in the body, then stand the duck up on the base where you want to mount it. Mark the locations of the legs on the base, then drill the holes.

You must also drill:

- ¼"-diameter holes through the feet of the duck
- ¼"-diameter, ½"-deep holes in the body of the duck, to hold the legs
- ¼"-diameter, ¼"-deep holes in the large base, to hold the other end of the legs (See Figure 3.)
- 3/16"-diameter holes through the feet of the ducklings
- 3/16"-diameter, ¼"-deep holes in the body of the ducklings, to hold the legs
- 3/16"-diameter, ¼"-deep holes in the small bases, to hold the other end of the legs (See Figure 3.)

———— ❖ ————

5. Assemble the duck and ducklings. Sand all the wooden parts smooth, then glue the wings to the bodies. Let the glue set and attach the legs to the bodies. Put the legs through the feet, and apply glue to the bottom ends of the legs and the bottom surfaces of the feet. Insert the legs in the base, positioning the feet so they face forward.

———— ❖ ————

6. Paint the duck and ducklings. Round the edges with a file and sandpaper to remove any sharp corners. Sand the wooden surfaces clean, then paint the duck, ducklings, and bases. Follow the suggested color scheme or invent your own.

———— ❖ ————

Colors Shown:

1. OFF WHITE
2. SUNKISS YELLOW
3. PURE ORANGE
4. SOFT BLACK

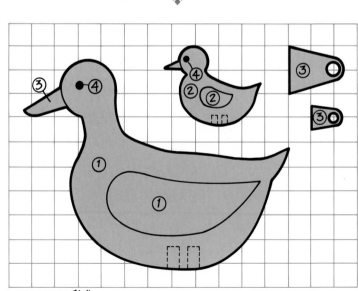

1 SQUARE = ½"

DUCK AND DUCKLING PATTERNS

7. Attach the wheels, pull cord, and bead. Mount the wheels, driving the axle nails into the bases as described in step 7 for the horse and pig pull toys. Cut a 24" length of nylon rope to make the pull cord, and attach it to the bead and duck base as described in step 7 for the horse and pig pull toys. Paint or apply a finish to the bead.

8. Tie the bases together. Cut three 6" lengths of rope and tie a knot in one end of each length. Thread the rope through the 3/16"-diameter holes near the *back* end of the duck base and two of the duckling bases. Pull the ropes through so the knots nest in the recesses, as you did for the pull cord. Then thread the other ends of the ropes through the 3/16"-diameter holes in the *front* ends of the three duckling bases. Tie knots in the ropes and nest the knots in the recesses.

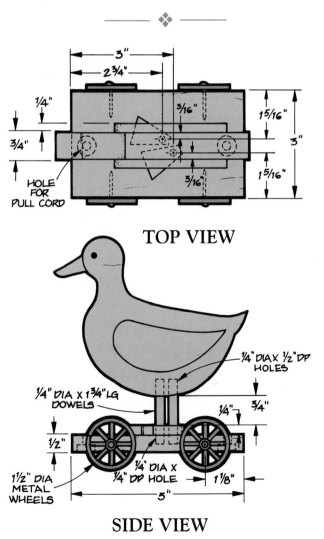

NOAH'S ARK

emember the Sabbath day," begins the Third Commandment (Exodus 20:8–11), "to keep it holy…thou shalt not do any work; thou, nor thy son, nor thy daughter…" Country folk took these words to heart. Sunday was a day of rest and reflection for the entire family — adults and children. To help their offspring make it through the day in good spiritual standing, parents gave them special "Sunday toys." These playthings were designed to discourage boisterous play and to keep the children peacefully occupied.

Miniature arks filled with animals were especially popular Sunday toys because they inspired quiet play and they had a biblical theme. Most arks and animal sets were imported from Europe, but many were made by loving parents or grandparents. The ark and animals shown are patterned after an old handmade set. The ark is a simple wooden box in the shape of a boat, and the animals are flat cutouts.

CUTTING LIST

Ark

A.	Bottom	½" x 7" x 10⅞"
B.	Sides (2)	½" x 4¾" x 17¼"
C.	Front/back (2)	½" x 7" x 7½"
D.	Deck	½" x 7" x 15"
E.	Bow	½" x 1½" x 7⅝"
F.	Rudder	½" x 2" x 7⅛"
G.	Cabin front/back (2)	½" x 5" x 5⅞"
H.	Cabin sides (2)	½" x 3⅞" x 8"
J.	Roof halves (2)	½" x 4½" x 11"
K.	Roof braces (2)	½" x 3" x 4"
L.	Mast	⅜" diameter x 11"
M.	Spar	¼" diameter x 2½"
N.	Wooden bead	¾" diameter

Figures

A.	Noah	¼" x 1½" x 2¾"
B.	Noah's base	¼" x ¾" x 1½"
C.	Mrs. Noah	¼" x 1" x 2¾"
D.	Mrs. Noah's base	¼" x ¾" x 1¼"
E.	Elephants (2)	¼" x 4½" x 5¼"
F.	Elephants' bases (2)	¼" x 1" x 3½"
G.	Giraffes (2)	¼" x 2¾" x 4⅞"
H.	Giraffes' bases (2)	¼" x 1" x 2¼"
J.	Elk bull	¼" x 2⅞" x 3¼"
K.	Elk cow	¼" x 2¾" x 2¾"
L.	Elks' bases (2)	¼" x ¾" x 2¼"
M.	Camels (2)	¼" x 2⅝" x 2⅞"
N.	Camels' bases (2)	¼" x ¾" x 2¼"
P.	Lion	¼" x 2⅛" x 4"
Q.	Lioness	¼" x 1¾" x 4"
R.	Lions' bases (2)	¼" x ¾" x 3¼"
S.	Zebras (2)	¼" x 2⅞" x 2⅞"
T.	Zebras' bases (2)	¼" x ¾" x 2½"
U.	Bears (2)	¼" x 2" x 2⅞"
V.	Bears' bases (2)	¼" x ¾" x 2⅜"
W.	Tigers (2)	¼" x 1¾" x 3¾"
X.	Tigers' bases (2)	¼" x ¾" x 3"
Y.	Kangaroos (2)	¼" x 2" x 2¾"
Z.	Kangaroos' bases (2)	¼" x ¾" x 2⅜"
AA.	Ostriches (2)	¼" x 1¾" x 3"
BB.	Ostriches' bases (2)	¼" x ¾" x 1¼"
CC.	Turtles (2)	¼" x 1" x 2¾"
DD.	Turtles' bases (2)	¼" x ¾" x 2¼"
EE.	Alligators (2)	¼" x ⅞" x 5½"
FF.	Alligators' bases (2)	¼" x ¾" x 4"
GG.	Goats (2)	¼" x 1¾" x 2¼"
HH.	Goats' bases (2)	¼" x ¾" x 1⅝"
JJ.	Swans (2)	¼" x 1½" x 1½"
KK.	Swans' bases (2)	¼" x ¾" x 1"
LL.	Foxes (2)	¼" x 1⅛" x 2¼"
MM.	Foxes' bases (2)	¼" x ¾" x 1⅜"
NN.	Snakes (2)	¼" x ¾" x 2⅛"
PP.	Snakes' bases (2)	¼" x ¾" x 1⅞"
QQ.	Skunks (2)	¼" x ⅞" x 1¼"
RR.	Skunks' bases (2)	¼" x ⅝" x ⅞"
SS.	Skunk boat sides	¾" x 1⅞" x 3¼"
TT.	Skunk boat bottom	¼" x 1⅞" x 3¼"
UU.	Doves (2)	¼" x ¾" x ⅞"
VV.	Doves' mounting dowels (2)	⅛" diameter x ¾"

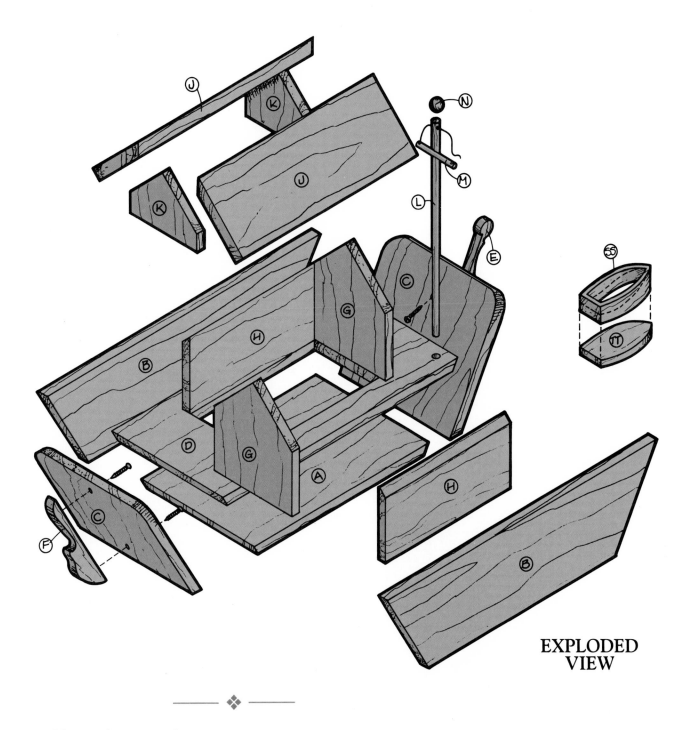

EXPLODED
VIEW

❖

1. Choose the materials. The roof of the ark fits the cabin like the
lid of a cookie jar, so select a very stable stock for the ark — one that
doesn't expand and contract too much with changes in humidity —
otherwise, the lid may stick. And since the ark will be painted, choose a
light-colored wood. Paint will cover white or cream-colored stock more
easily than a darker wood. Soft maple, poplar, and white pine are good
choices — they're all stable, light-colored, and easy to work.

The animals should be cut from plywood. If you make them from solid wood, the ears, legs, tails, and other protrusions may break off. When choosing plywood, look for light-colored woods that are rated "AB"; this will give you a good painting surface on both sides. Cabinet-grade, birch-veneer plywood is a good choice.

The dowels are available at most lumberyards and hardware stores. You can purchase the wooden bead at some lumberyards, crafts and hobby stores, or from mail-order woodworking suppliers. Refer to Appendix B for addresses.

❖

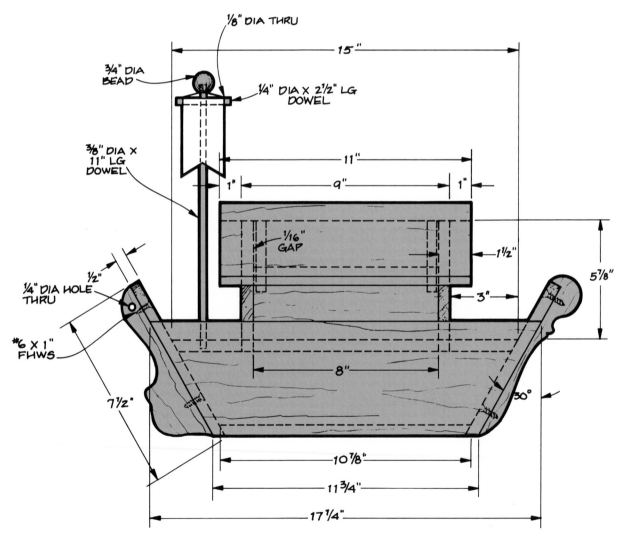

SIDE VIEW

2. Cut the parts of the ark to size. Cut the wooden parts of the ark to the sizes shown in the Cutting List. Cut the bow and the rudder slightly oversize, so you have room to cut their shape.

You must miter or bevel the edges and ends of several parts. Bevel-cut the bottom ends of the ark front and back, and both ends of the bottom and the deck at 30°. Bevel-cut the top edges of the cabin sides and the roof halves at 45°. Cut the bevels with a saber saw, tilting the base to the necessary angle. (See Figure 1.)

Miter the sides at 30°, and the cabin front, back, and roof braces at 45°. However, don't cut these miters yet; just mark them. Dry-assemble the ark front, back, bottom, and deck, laying the assembly in place on one of the sides. Check that you have properly positioned the marks for the miters: the mitered ends of the sides must line up with the ark's front and back. If not, make new marks for the miters.

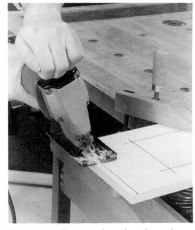

Figure 1. To saw a bevel with a saber saw, tilt the base of the saw to the required angle. Cut slowly and carefully. To make the cut as straight as possible, clamp a straightedge to the stock to help guide the saw.

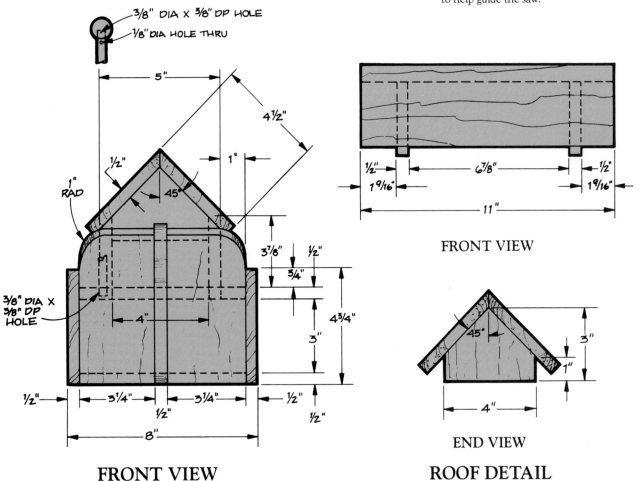

FRONT VIEW

FRONT VIEW

END VIEW

ROOF DETAIL

Do the same for the cabin. Dry-assemble the front, back, and sides, then check that the beveled edges of the sides line up with the miters marked on the front and back. Finally, check the roof braces. Put the beveled edges of the roof halves together and place them end-up on a roof brace. The miter marks should line up with the underside of the roof halves.

When you're satisfied that all the miters are properly marked, cut them with a handsaw or saber saw. (Readjust the base of the saw to 0° *before* you cut the miters.)

— ❖ —

3. Cut the ark shapes. Trace the Bow Pattern and the Rudder Pattern onto ½"-thick stock, and the Skunk Boat/Top View onto ¼"- and ¾"-thick stock. Cut out the shapes with a saber saw. Also round the top corners of the ark front and back, as shown in the Front View. Sand the edges smooth.

— ❖ —

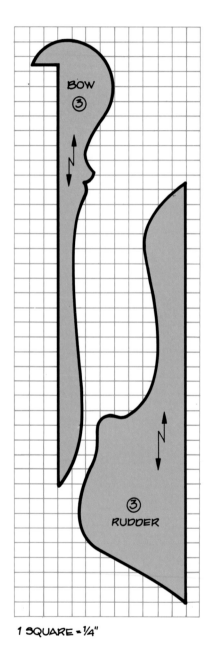

BOW AND RUDDER PATTERNS

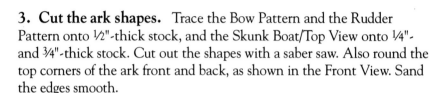

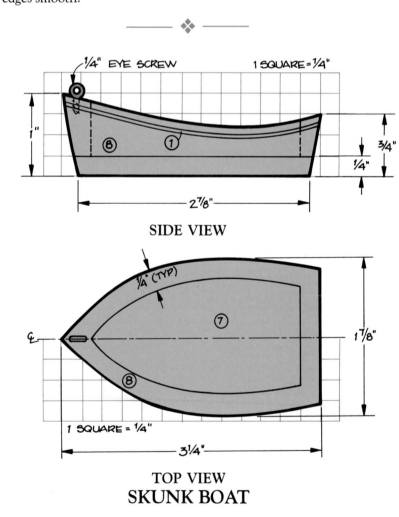

TOP VIEW SKUNK BOAT

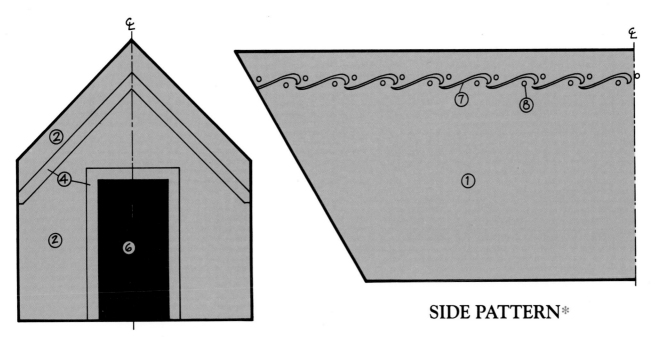

FRONT PATTERN＊

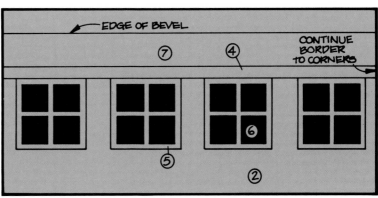

SIDE PATTERN＊

EDGE OF BEVEL

⑦ ④

CONTINUE
BORDER
TO CORNERS

⑤

⑥

②

SIDE PATTERN＊

1" RAD
+

①

END PATTERN＊

＊ALL PATTERNS
ON THIS PAGE
ARE HALF-SIZE.

Colors Shown:

① CHESAPEAKE BLUE
② PEACHES N' CREAM
③ SOFT BLUE
④ EQUAL PARTS PARADISE
   BLUE AND OFF WHITE
⑤ OFF WHITE
⑥ EQUAL PARTS SOLDIER
   BLUE AND GREEN OLIVE
⑦ L'ORANGERIE
⑧ EQUAL PARTS DIJON GOLD
   AND PENNSYLVANIA CLAY

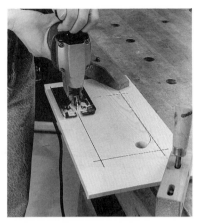

Figure 2. To make the access opening in the deck, you must first drill a starting hole, then saw outward from this hole, cutting the shape of the opening. This technique is called piercing.

4. Cut the deck access and the skunk boat opening. The deck is cut away beneath the cabin, allowing access to the hull of the ark to store the animals. Mark the access opening on the deck, as shown in the Deck Layout. Drill a ¾"-diameter hole inside the outline of the opening. Insert the blade of a saber saw or coping saw through the hole, and cut to the outline. Continue cutting, following the outline, until the waste is free. Sand the sawed edges of the opening. (See Figure 2.)

Make the skunk boat opening using the same technique. Mark the inside outline of the sides, as shown in the Skunk Boat/Top View on the ¾"-thick stock. (You've already cut the outside shape.) Drill a hole in the waste, insert the saw blade, and cut out the waste. Sand the sawed edges.

❖

5. Drill the holes. Drill the holes you need to mount the mast and the bead, and to hang the spar:

- ⅜"-diameter hole, ⅜" deep, in the deck, as shown in the Deck Layout
- ⅜"-diameter hole, ⅜" deep, in the wooden bead to mount it on the mast (See Figure 3.)
- ¼"-diameter hole through the rudder, near the top, to tie the skunk boat
- ⅛" holes through the upper end of the mast and through both ends of the spar

❖

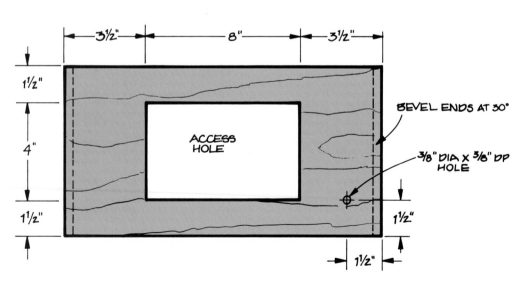

DECK LAYOUT

6. Assemble the ark. Finish-sand the parts of the ark, then assemble them in the order described below. Use wire brads and glue to secure each joint, unless otherwise directed.

Attach the cabin front and back to the cabin sides. Center the cabin assembly over the access opening in the deck, and attach it to the deck.

Attach the bow to the front, and the rudder to the back with glue and flathead screws. Drive the screws through the front or back and into the shaped parts. Countersink the screw heads flush with the wood surface.

Assemble the front, back, and deck assemblies, and the bottom. Then attach the sides to complete the hull.

Assemble the roof halves and roof braces. Carefully position the braces so they'll fit inside the cabin front and back. When the roof is in place, there should be a tiny gap between the braces and the cabin, as shown in the Side View. This will keep the roof assembly from binding when it's removed or replaced.

Finally, glue the wooden bead to the mast. *Don't* glue the mast in the deck. Leave it loose so you can store the mast in the hull with the animals when you put the ark away.

As you work, use a wet rag to wipe away any glue that squeezes out of the joints. Also, set the heads of the brads slightly below the surface of the wood with a nail punch. When the glue dries, sand all the joints clean and, wherever necessary, sand the wooden surfaces flush.

Figure 3. To keep the wooden bead from rolling around when you drill it, first drill a ⅝"-diameter hole in a scrap of wood. Place the bead in the hole, then drill a ⅜" hole in the bead.

7. Assemble and shape the skunk boat. Glue the skunk boat sides to the boat bottom. Wait for the glue to dry, then shape the boat with a rasp and sandpaper. Taper the sides and put a slight curve in the top edges, as shown in the Skunk Boat/Side View. Install a small eye screw in the bow.

8. Cut the shapes of the animals. Trace the animal shapes on the plywood. (Remember, you'll need *two* of each animal.) If you cut the shapes by hand, use a coping saw. If you cut them with a saber saw, mount a scrolling blade in the power tool. Scrolling blades are small and have many tiny teeth. The small blade enables you to cut detailed shapes, and the teeth won't chip or tear the plywood. After cutting the shapes, sand or file the edges smooth.

NOAH

OSTRICH

ZEBRA

SKUNK

MRS. NOAH

ELEPHANT

1 SQUARE = ¼"

FIGURE PATTERNS (FULL SIZE)

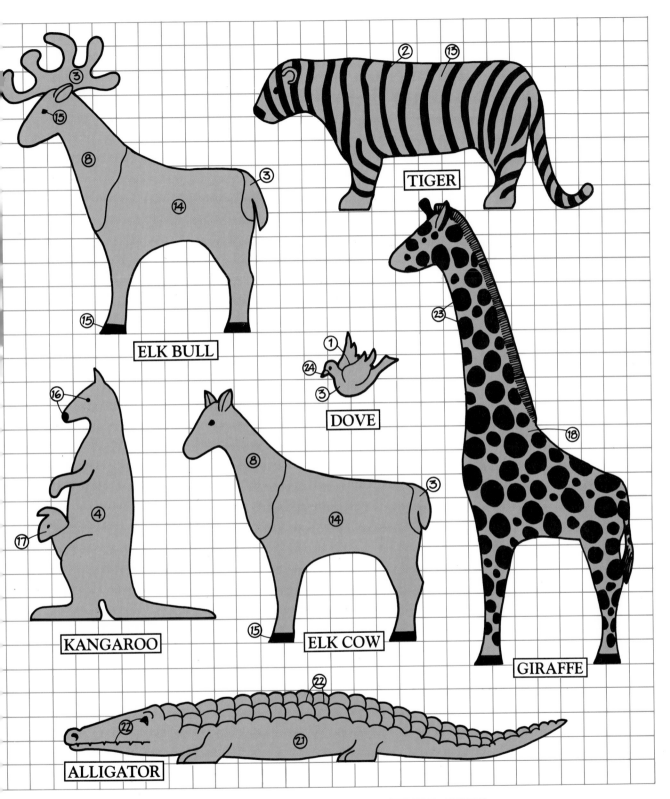

FIGURE PATTERNS (FULL SIZE)

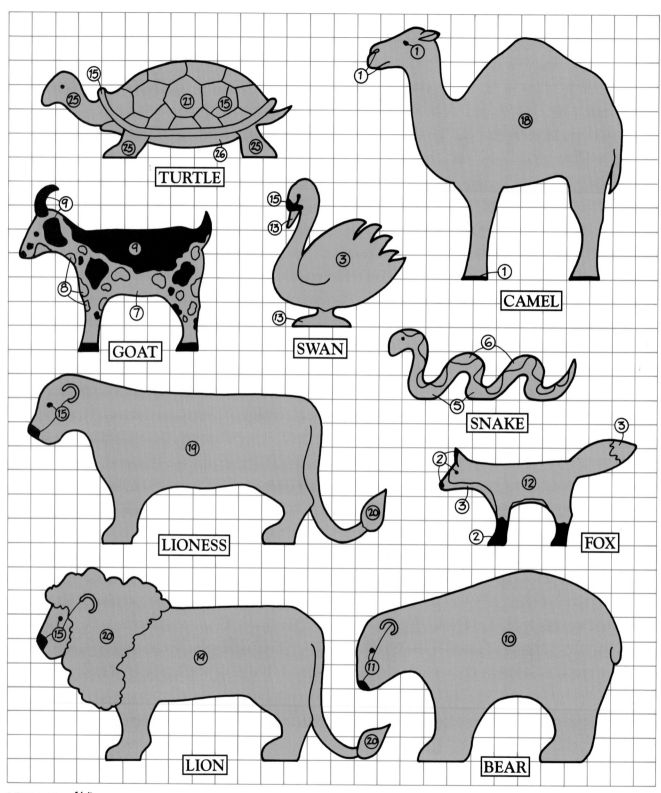

FIGURE PATTERNS (FULL SIZE)

1 SQUARE = ¼"

9. Mount the animals on bases. Cut the bases from ¼"-thick stock and sand all the surfaces. Carefully mark which base goes with what animal, so you don't get them mixed up.

Center each animal on its base, and mark the positions of the feet. Drill ³⁄₃₂"-diameter holes through the base where the feet touch, then position the animal's feet over the holes and attach the animal to the base with epoxy glue. Let the glue set for 24 hours. Using the holes that you've already drilled as guides, and a ³⁄₃₂"-diameter drill bit, drill up through the base and about ½" into the animal's feet. Dip the point of a toothpick in carpenter's glue, and insert a toothpick up into each hole — the toothpicks serve as pegs to help secure the animal to the base and hold it upright. When the glue sets, break off the protruding portions of the toothpicks and sand them flush with the undersurface of the base. (See Figures 4 through 8.) Repeat for each animal.

Figure 4. To attach an animal to its base, first mark the position of the feet on the base.

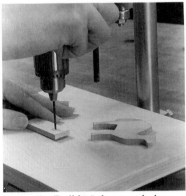

Figure 5. Drill ³⁄₃₂"-diameter holes through the base, at the points where the feet will be attached.

Figure 6. Attach the animal to the base, directly over the holes you just drilled, using epoxy glue. Tape the animal and base to a scrap board, as shown, to keep it upright while the glue sets.

Colors Shown:

①	EQUAL PARTS STONEWARE BLUE AND ANTIQUE WHITE	⑯	EQUAL PARTS RAW UMBER AND FLESH
②	SOFT BLACK	⑰	EQUAL PARTS PARADISE BLUE AND STONEWARE BLUE
③	OFF WHITE	⑱	EQUAL PARTS GOLDEN HARVEST AND INDIAN SKY
④	EQUAL PARTS SOLDIER BLUE AND WILD HONEY	⑲	EQUAL PARTS GOLDEN HARVEST AND PEACHES N' CREAM
⑤	EQUAL PARTS GREEN APPLE AND PARADISE BLUE	⑳	SEDONA CLAY
⑥	EQUAL PARTS PRAIRIE GREEN AND GREEN APPLE	㉑	EQUAL PARTS GREEN OLIVE AND GREEN APPLE
⑦	ANTIQUE WHITE	㉒	EQUAL PARTS SOLDIER BLUE AND GREEN OLIVE
⑧	EQUAL PARTS GOLDEN HARVEST AND PENNSYLVANIA CLAY	㉓	PENNSYLVANIA CLAY
⑨	EQUAL PARTS GREEN APPLE AND PENNSYLVANIA CLAY	㉔	L'ORANGERIE
⑩	EQUAL PARTS BURNT UMBER AND BARN RED	㉕	GREEN APPLE
⑪	RAW UMBER	㉖	EQUAL PARTS CHESAPEAKE BLUE AND PEACHES N' CREAM
⑫	EQUAL PARTS L'ORANGERIE AND PEACHES N' CREAM	㉗	EQUAL PARTS OFF WHITE AND PENNSYLVANIA CLAY
⑬	EQUAL PARTS L'ORANGERIE AND DIJON GOLD	㉘	EQUAL PARTS SEDONA CLAY AND ANTIQUE WHITE
⑭	EQUAL PARTS WILD HONEY AND PEACHES N' CREAM	㉙	RAW SIENNA
⑮	BURNT UMBER	㉚	EQUAL PARTS GREEN APPLE AND CHESAPEAKE BLUE
		㉛	BARN RED

Figure 7. Allow the glue to harden overnight, then using the ³⁄₃₂"-diameter holes you drilled previously as guides, drill ³⁄₃₂"-diameter holes up through the base and into the animal's feet.

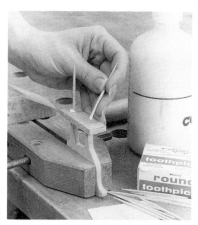

Figure 8. Use toothpicks as pegs to secure the animal on its base. Dip the point of each toothpick in carpenter's glue and insert it in a hole. When the glue sets, break off the toothpicks and sand them flush with the bottom surface of the base.

Before you attach Noah to his base, drill a ³⁄₃₂"-diameter hole through his hand. After you've mounted him, bend a small length of 12-gauge copper wire in the shape of a shepherd's crook and insert it through the hole in Noah's hand. Put a dab of epoxy glue where the crook goes through the hand, and another where the crook rests against the base. This will secure the crook.

Instead of mounting the doves on bases, drill a ⅛"-diameter, ⅜"-deep hole in the bottom edge of each bird and glue a dowel in the hole. Then drill two ⅛"-diameter, ⅜"-deep holes in the roof of the ark, near the peak, about 1" apart. Insert the free end of the dowels in the holes (but *don't* glue them), mounting the doves on the roof.

10. Paint the animals and the ark. Paint the animals and the ark as suggested or make up your own color scheme. You may want to borrow some picture books of animals from the local library to use as guides. If you wish, apply a protective coat of clear varnish or polyurethane to the painted surfaces, particularly if children will use the ark as a toy.

11. Make and hang the banner. Cut the banner to the shape shown in the Banner Pattern, then trace the design on the canvas. Paint the banner, using the same acrylic paints that you used on the wooden parts. You don't have to hem the edges of the banner — the paint should be thick enough to act as a sizing and keep the canvas from unraveling.

When the paint dries, fold the top end of the banner over the spar and glue the folded portion to the back of the banner. Tie a knot in one end of a 6" length of nylon string. Thread it up through one of the ⅛"-diameter holes in the spar, through the hole in the mast, then down through the other hole in the spar. Tie a knot in the other end of the string so it won't slip out of the holes, then trim the loose ends.

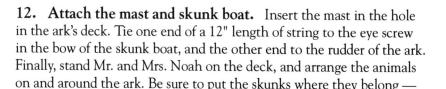

12. Attach the mast and skunk boat. Insert the mast in the hole in the ark's deck. Tie one end of a 12" length of string to the eye screw in the bow of the skunk boat, and the other end to the rudder of the ark. Finally, stand Mr. and Mrs. Noah on the deck, and arrange the animals on and around the ark. Be sure to put the skunks where they belong — in the skunk boat.

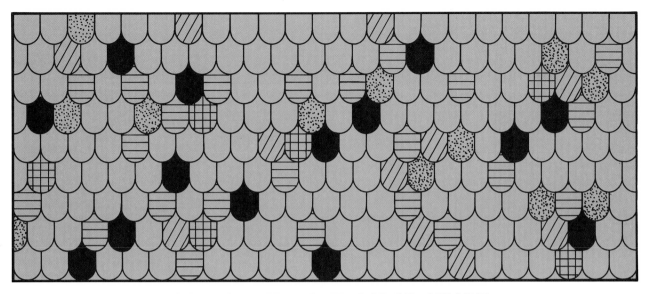

ROOF PATTERN AND COLOR CHART

BARN RED

EQUAL PARTS
SEDONA CLAY AND
DIJON GOLD

EQUAL PARTS
L'ORANGERIE AND
PENNSYLVANIA CLAY

BRICK

EQUAL PARTS
PENNSYLVANIA CLAY
AND PEACHES N' CREAM

PENNSYLVANIA
CLAY

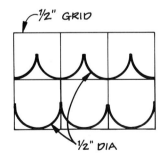

½" GRID

½" DIA

PATTERN
FOR
SHINGLE

Colors Shown:

① CHESAPEAKE BLUE
② EQUAL PARTS OFF WHITE
   AND PARADISE BLUE
③ L'ORANGERIE
④ EQUAL PARTS DIJON GOLD
   AND PENNSYLVANIA
   CLAY

FOLD LINE

③
①
④
① ② ①
①

1 SQUARE = ¼"

BANNER PATTERN

Appendix A: Color Chart

BORDEAUX

HOLIDAY RED

JOSONJA RED

PURE RED

APACHE RED

BARN RED

TRUE ORANGE

COTTAGE ROSE

ROSEBERRY

VICTORIAN MAUVE

PENNSYLVANIA CLAY

L'ORANGERIE

APRICOT STONE

PEACHES N' CREAM

FLESH

SEDONA CLAY

DIJON GOLD

SUNKISS YELLOW

CACTUS FLOWER

OFF WHITE

BRICK

GOLDEN HARVEST

ANTIQUE WHITE

WILD HONEY

WHITE WASH

MUSTARD SEED

WICKER

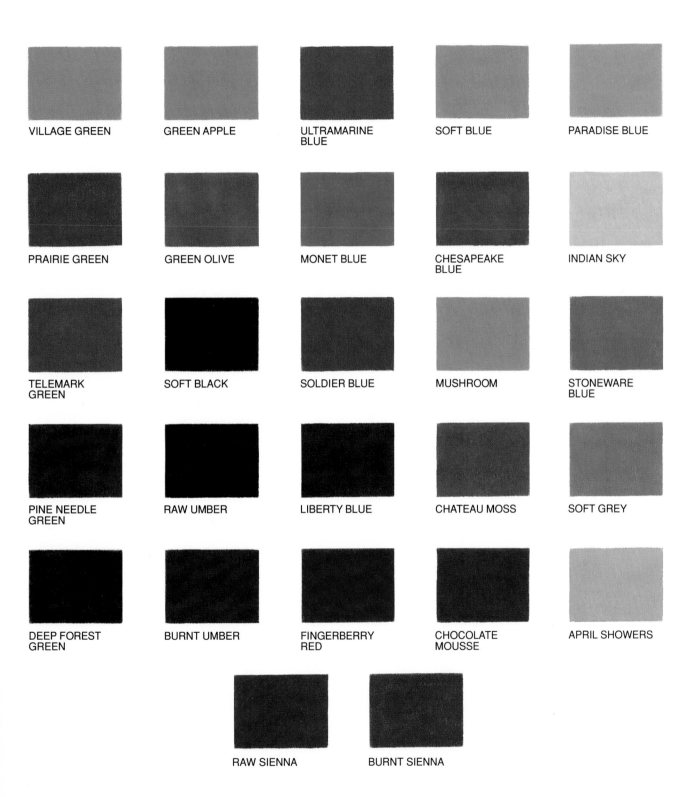

VILLAGE GREEN

GREEN APPLE

ULTRAMARINE
BLUE

SOFT BLUE

PARADISE BLUE

PRAIRIE GREEN

GREEN OLIVE

MONET BLUE

CHESAPEAKE
BLUE

INDIAN SKY

TELEMARK
GREEN

SOFT BLACK

SOLDIER BLUE

MUSHROOM

STONEWARE
BLUE

PINE NEEDLE
GREEN

RAW UMBER

LIBERTY BLUE

CHATEAU MOSS

SOFT GREY

DEEP FOREST
GREEN

BURNT UMBER

FINGERBERRY
RED

CHOCOLATE
MOUSSE

APRIL SHOWERS

RAW SIENNA

BURNT SIENNA

Appendix B: Source List

Company	Product
Cherry Tree Toys, Inc. P.O. Box 369 Belmont, OH 43718	Toy parts, small wooden parts, small hardware, woodworking kits, plans
Constantine's 2050 Eastchester Road Bronx, NY 10461	Wood, tools, woodworking supplies
Country Colors Illinois Bronze Paint Company Lake Zurich, IL 60047	Acrylic paints
Craftsman Wood Service 1735 W. Cortland Court Addison, IL 60101	Wood, tools, woodworking supplies
Eisenbrand Hardwoods, Inc. 4100 Spencer Street Torrance, CA 90503	Wood
Garrett Wade 161 Avenue of the Americas New York, NY 10013	Tools, hardware, woodworking supplies
Horton Brasses Nooks Hill Road P.O. Box 120V Cromwell, CT 06416	Brass hardware
Klockit P.O. Box 629 Lake Geneva, WI 53147	Clock parts and kits
Leichtung Workshops 4944 Commerce Parkway Cleveland, OH 44128	Tools, hardware, woodworking supplies
Mason & Sullivan 586 Higgins Crowell Road West Yarmouth, MA 02673	Clock parts and kits
Meisal Hardware Specialties P.O. Box 70 Mound, MN 55364	Small wooden parts, hardware, woodworking supplies
Native American Hardwoods Box 6484 West Valley, NY 14171	Wood
Shaker Workshops P.O. Box 1028 Concord, MA 01742	Pegs, finishing materials, furniture kits
Shopsmith, Inc. 6640 Poe Avenue Dayton, OH 45414	Tools, woodworking supplies
St. Croix Kits 423 South Main Stillwater, MN 55082	Musical instrument parts and kits
Stewart-MacDonald Mfg. Box 900 Athens, OH 45701	Musical instrument parts and kits
Timbers Woodworking Timbers Building Carnelian Bay, CA 95711	Small wooden parts, kits, and plans
The Wise Company 6503 St. Claude Avenue Arabi, LA 70032	Hardware
Woodcraft 210 Wood County Industrial Park P.O. Box 1686 Parkersburg, WV 26102	Wood, tools, and woodworking supplies
Woodcraft 41 Atlantic Avenue P.O. Box 4000 Woburn, MA 01888	Tool, hardware, woodworking supplies
Wood Finishing Supply Co. 1267 Mary Drive Macedon, NY 14502	Wood finishes
The Woodworker's Store 21801 Industrial Boulevard Rogers, MN 55374	Tools, hardware, woodworking supplies
Woodworker's Supply 5604 Alameda Place Albuquerque, NM 87113	Tools, hardware, woodworking supplies
Woodworks 4013-A Clay Avenue Fort Worth, TX 76117	Small wooden parts

Index

All of us at Sedgewood® Press are dedicated to offering you, our customer, the best books we can create. We are particularly concerned that all of the instructions for making the projects are clear and accurate. We welcome your comments and would like to hear any suggestions you may have. Please address your correspondence to Customer Service Department, Sedgewood® Press, Meredith Corporation, 750 Third Avenue, New York, NY 10017.

For information on how you can have *Better Homes and Gardens* delivered to your door, write to: Mr. Robert Austin, P. O. Box 4536, Des Moines, IA 50336.